People Who Lunch

People Who Lunch

On Work, Leisure, and Loose Living

Sally Olds

Little, Brown Spark
New York   Boston   London

Little, Brown Spark
Hachette Book Group
1290 Avenue of the Americas, New York, NY 10104
littlebrownspark.com

First North American Edition: February 2024
Originally published in Australia by Upswell Publishing, August 2022

Little, Brown Spark is an imprint of Little, Brown and Company, a division of Hachette Book Group, Inc. The Little, Brown Spark name and logo are trademarks of Hachette Book Group, Inc.

The publisher is not responsible for websites (or their content) that are not owned by the publisher.

The Hachette Speakers Bureau provides a wide range of authors for speaking events. To find out more, go to hachettespeakersbureau.com or email HachetteSpeakers@hbgusa.com.

Little, Brown and Company books may be purchased in bulk for business, educational, or promotional use. For information, please contact your local bookseller or the Hachette Book Group Special Markets Department at special.markets@hbgusa.com.

ISBN 9780316565714
LCCN 2023944050

Printing 1, 2023

LSC-C

Printed in the United States of America

Contents

For Kat

Introduction to the US Edition

I started writing *People Who Lunch* in 2017, when I moved from Brisbane to Melbourne to do postgraduate study at one of the universities here. For two years, I was funded to do an MA, which—since this is for an American audience, I'll explain—is sort of like an MFA but free, and without the writing workshops or dubious prestige. I had a small, shared office, a supervisor I met with regularly, and a building full of writers and researchers to talk to or avoid as the mood struck. I wrote the first draft of three of these essays during this time. I woke up, chatted with my housemates, walked to my office, and read books. The campus was sandstone and leafy, with rolling green lawns on which students smoked and canoodled in the sunshine. I felt I was living in the novel *The Secret History*, but a version of it where things went well. Before this period of calm, expansive time, I had worked casual jobs continuously since I was fourteen. My new circumstances informed what I read and how I read it. When Rene Ricard wrote, "I've never worked a day in my life. If I did it would probably ruin my career," I knew instantly what he meant. I nodded when Ottessa Moshfegh made her claim about writing *Eileen* to the formula of a bestseller in order to lift herself out of working menial jobs. I misread Franco "Bifo" Berardi's concept of "refusal of work" to mean that people, people like me, should simply refuse to work.

Introduction to the US Edition

I studiously underlined Marx's line about how capital comes into the world dripping "with blood and dirt."

I had these two years of respite, but on the other side of them I could see the rest of my life stretched out ahead of me, job after job after boring job. There was always Centrelink, I figured — Australia's social security system, which pays you a below-poverty-level wage if you become unemployed. Centrelink is how a lot of Australia's best books managed to get written. Many Australian books feature Centrelink in some way, explicitly or in the background, the reason the characters are eating, drinking, and smoking without working too much. (The same thing they say about New York City applies to Centrelink — it's like Centrelink is another character in Australian books.) It explains a lot of the people in this book, the specific class position of being broke but with a government-supplied safety net. Many of the people in the book are also artists of some kind. This is not a coincidence. The overlap between welfare and the arts is so fundamental in Australia that it has furnished a national cliché — that all artists are dole-bludging layabouts.

I'm not here to contest that; I'm here to enjoy it while it lasts. I've heard that to make art in America you have to be rich or have rich parents (which amounts to the same thing). Americans, is that true? Do your artists have jobs? How did, say, *Infinite Jest* get written? The truth is, in Australia, we are hot on the heels of US-style immiseration. When I showed this introduction to a friend, he laughed at the parts about university. He reminded me that during this time, when we both taught undergraduate classes to supplement our stipends, we, along with a few hundred other casual staff, rallied outside the vice chancellor's own private mansion in order to drive home a point about wage theft. I had forgotten about the whole stolen wages thing. I had also forgotten that the uni turned our offices into hot desks, that I'd arrived at our room one morning to find myself suddenly locked out. He reminded me, too, that Centrelink is a slog. To get on the dole, you have to fill out endless forms, you have to attend meetings every two weeks, and you can be docked payments if you fail to complete these tasks. So let me refine the above. It is more accurate to say that many of the people in this book fall within the specific class position of being broke but with a government-supplied safety net that may be yanked away at any moment. Maintaining the safety net — and dodging the many varieties of soul-crushing jobs out there — requires constant, disruptive, unsexy exertions; while writing this book, I spent a lot of my lunch breaks at grindingly slow union meetings.

Sure enough, at the end of this time, I went on and off Centrelink and cycled through a few jobs while working on the book. What I wound up with is *People Who Lunch*, a book of essays that were (that are) some attempts to think myself and others out of this raw deal, of working to barely make ends meet. It is my first book. It is not a political treatise, a book of hard theory, or a guide of any kind. It is a series of tasks I set myself for the fun of it, a way of sending myself out into the world to talk to people and go places. Money is a shorthand for aspiration, and so I write about how people get money (an incomplete list from the book: cryptocurrency, sex work, welfare, property, arts grants, café jobs, truck driving), but I also write about aspirations cut loose from money and rerouted to stranger ends. An archaic secret society strives to preserve itself and grows rich in the process; utopian polyamorists model their relationships in the image of a classless society; amateur cryptocurrency investors dream of white-picket fences. I've been told more than once that it's a "very Melbourne book" (double-edged praise, for sure), but a lot of it comes from elsewhere, too: the Venice Biennale, communes in California, and regional Queensland, where I grew up. And although I wrote the bulk of it in Australia, I made the very final edits in New York City.

I'm not sure if people in America know this, but Australia has a strange, tortured relationship to America, and Melbourne in particular has a strange, tortured relationship to New York. If you're a writer from Melbourne, you might dream of moving to New York to make it big, or you might hate New York with a passion because it represents the imperialist center of the writing world, the thing that makes it nearly impossible to succeed as an Australian writer (let alone one *not* from a minor colonial power). Most people who think about such things feel both ways at the same time. It's like Melbourne is a bit obsessed with New York, but maybe New York doesn't even know we exist? I could have told you where to go clubbing on the Lower East Side long before I'd ever set foot in Manhattan, but I know from being there that Manhattanites still cock their heads and say, "Mell-borrn, is that near the beach?" This is humbling for a city that thinks of itself as the New York of Australia. (Sydney is our LA, by the way.) So it felt fitting to be in New York for the first time in my life while finishing the book, a book about fantasies and delusions and marginal, doomed endeavors: to be at the center of all this angst and striving.

When I settled on *People Who Lunch* as the title, I was, in fact, thinking about Truman Capote's unfinished novel *Answered Prayers*, or the excerpt published in *Esquire* in 1975 that lost him all his friends. The excerpt, titled "La Côte Basque, 1965," is an exposing portrait, barely veiled, of Capote's companions: New York City society ladies who lunch. A representative passage goes like this: "The Cristal was being poured. Ina tasted it. 'It's not cold enough. But ahhh!' She swallowed again. 'I do miss Cole. And Howard Sturgis. Even Papa; after all, he did write about me in *Green Hills of Africa...*'" This is how Capote moves the story along: "She swallowed again." Between each swig of champagne, there are approximately thirty proper nouns. Everyone is called something like Teddie or Dixie or Babe or is a princess with a seven-part compound name. The climax of the story is the revelation that one of the ladies is a murderess. Honestly — very chic. Then the soufflé arrives. There is purse seizing, dramatic nose powdering. Jackie Kennedy sweeps past. You can practically hear the rustle of stiff silk. More Cristal is poured. You wonder if Truman was sponsored by Bulgari, or at least the CIA.

In New York, I visited the Wall Street Bull, rode helmet-less through Central Park (another difference: Melbourne's e-scooters and city bikes all come with helmets, and helmet-wearing is mandated by law), and had exactly one decadent meal. I quickly realized that to experience decadence in New York City with any regularity you would probably have to be Kennedy-level wealthy, and definitely not in possession of an Australian bank account worth sixty-seven cents on the US dollar. La Côte Basque closed years ago, so I went to another famous French brasserie (though it was for dinner, not lunch), dutifully ate my *steak frites*, and watched a group of nineteen-year-olds at the table next to us, grandchildren of the Teddies and Dixies and Babes they couldn't imprison for tax crimes. They were picking at their snails and lettuce salads, slumping on each other's shoulders, getting up and knocking over chairs and switching places, giggling, all of them glowing in the dewy skins of wealth and youth. Outside, a few blocks up, big white trailers like refrigerators lined the street, humming, the cast of the rebooted *Gossip Girl* incubating inside.

In New York, I thought about the difference between *people* and *ladies*. The people in my book are not ladies, not like Truman Capote's lunch set. Rather, they are people aspiring to be *ladies*, if *ladies* here is a placeholder for the Teddies and Dixies and Babes of the world, for ladies of leisure, people of leisure — for anyone who never has to work. I thought about how being on Centrelink or writing a book can be a way to play make-believe with leisure, to approximate the lifestyle of a lady who lunches, even if upholding the fantasy is an enormous labor in itself. I thought about how, when I don't know what I want, or when I want something abstract, my desire latches onto something concrete, something ready-made and usually much more banal — like I start out wanting quote unquote a better world and wind up in a Zara cubicle trying on blazers.

Back in Melbourne, a year or so on from the book's Australian publication, I'm no closer to quitting my day job, and we are no closer to ending wage labor. Certain questions in the book remain unanswered: Who is George Cooper Murray? What was Dr. Young doing with those prairie voles? Where do you go to get a drink in this city after 1 a.m.? Certain throughlines, whole sections of argument and inquiry, are now nearly impossible for me to access in the same way I once did, a result of the weird dulling that happens once you've read your own work fifty or more times. Now, when I read *People Who Lunch*, what I get from the essays is a sense of energy, my own, which in real life flags often and drastically, but which in the book feels boundless. I never like it when people oppose utopian dreaming to cold, hard reality. You always know which one's going to come out on top; it's a plot arc that only goes one way. In the essays what I feel now is the energy of idealism meeting reality, and, in a happy twist, finding the two to be perfectly entwined. Sure, sometimes the people in my book dream big, and it doesn't work out. But by then the dream has already structured their realities, or was always at the center of them, the deep, wormy soil from which everything grows. I see myself in *People Who Lunch* charting a material world — of shoes, buildings, designer dogs — but a world that is nevertheless saturated with ideas and ideals: an intelligent, fanciful concoction. It's not a charmed world, by any means. It's complicated. But for me, at least, spending time with this complexity has been its own reward.

For Discussion and Resolution

I am writing this on an Australian Government Research Training Program Scholarship. I am sitting in the brown-wood office I share with four other postgraduate students, staring at the detritus of academia: a stack of back issues of the faculty journal; one bottle of Bacardi Gold, one bottle of Cointreau, one bottle of Smirnoff, eight shot glasses, nine plastic cups (no one knows where this stash came from or how old it is); eleven dusty boxes of tea bags, mostly expired; a statuette of a man in a crown; an orange plastic bucket with a Jack-o'-Lantern's face; one can of air freshener; two dead modems; one live mouse.

I am doing a research master's, which has no tuition fees. I receive $515.85 every week in exchange for... what, exactly? Showing up? The presumption that I will publish and provide the university with more citations, possibly acclaim? For giving the university an opportunity to support the universal right to education? I wonder what surplus I will produce in my time here.

So far I've been treating the scholarship more like a universal basic income than a wage in exchange for a product. I've been finishing projects I started during the three years between undergrad and postgrad in which I held down casual jobs. I've

9

been taking long lunches with friends who are likewise study-
ing, or underemployed, or jobless, or sex workers, or sessional
academics, or dole bludgers. Since I started in February I've
been suspended in the loophole between the job market and
unemployment that is tertiary education. It will end when I
graduate. Then maybe more study, a PhD, a relocation to claim
more funding, another loophole.

I am single partly in order to pursue more funding. There
was no money where my ex and I lived. He wanted to stay, I
wanted to move, and neither of us wanted to do monogamy by
distance. The other option was polyamory, but we had already
tried and it didn't work out. Does this mean I am pursuing funding in order to avoid being polyamorous?

I am pursuing funding partly in order to do the intellectual
labor that will help make a post-work future possible in order to
avoid the staggering exertions of holding down a poly setup
while also holding down an array of casual jobs. I am performing the intellectual labor of thinking through a post-work
future partly in order to gain funding.

Like many funded students and artists, I am already living
in a post-work future. I am pursuing funding in order to theo-
rize the conditions that might extend this from a temporary
state of grace to a permanent one.

*

In its loosest definition, what I call post-work polyamory is a
relationship form premised on and committed to anti-capitalism.
It is, or would be, a romantic, caring, and/or sexual relationship

between any number of people working against privatizing and unequally distributing care, resources, property, love, sex, intimacy, and work within a couple or other closed unit. It would be a form against the nuclear family as an atomized site of consumption and production. It does not see the couple form as inherently bad, but as a symptom of mononormativity: a state in which everything in society is calibrated for the monogamous pair. Its post-work ambitions are exactly what they sound like. Post-work polyamory does not just want to redistribute labor but, where possible, abolish the need to work within exploited waged (and unwaged) relations in order to survive.

These ambitions are nothing new, but polyamory today bears little resemblance to such a form. Researching polyamory — and I mean polyamory, not related forms like relationship anarchy or open relationships — is a frustrating experience of getting stuck within the very definitions I want to escape: poly as a 1990s/2000s urban North American spin on the 1970s version of free love, an orientation or practice for individuals, couples, and small groups, devoid of politics beyond its opposition to the monogamous status quo. The word "poly-amory" was only coined in 1990, by a witch, in a magazine with a tiny circulation among the pagan community in North America (more on this later); before this, polyamory, or its animating spirit, appears in many different guises and experiments. PWP has to invent its own predecessors, to arrange histories that don't quite belong to it in a shape that seems, in retrospect, to lead to something that could be called post-work polyamory.

*

Maybe Charles Fourier started it; at least, he demonstrates many of the same preoccupations as current-day poly people, most notably a deep and abiding love for organization. Born in 1772 in France, Fourier developed the idea of the *phalanstère* at the beginning of the 1800s as a counterpoint to the alienated living and working conditions he saw around him as he traveled Europe. The *phalanstère* is a self-sufficient property designed to house people of all classes, professions, talents, and ages. Each phalanx would consist of 1,620 people, 810 male, and 810 female. Fourier believed there were 810 different personality types, and so, as in Noah's Ark, there would be a male and female representative of each. Playing God? Absolutely. His philosophy of social life resembles an ambitiously plotted fantasy novel. He believed not so much in equality as in total variation. In the *phalanstère*, he wanted groups to form based on people's natural talents and interests — groups of farmers, artisans, gardeners, and more — but he also wanted rivalries to form within and between groups, spurring them on to greater achievements. Jobs would rotate between individuals and groups, as he believed people tire of doing the same work over and over again; and lovers could rotate, for the same reason. He was happy to admit wealthy men into the *phalanstère*, as long as they had different *amounts* of wealth.

Karl Marx he wasn't — but Marx did read Fourier, and in 1843 Marx and his wife, Jenny von Westphalen, moved to Paris to join a Fourierist urban commune. They moved in with two other couples and occupied two floors of an apartment at 23 rue Vaneau, Saint Germain. Each couple had their own quarters but shared a kitchen and dining room; the women did the domestic work, but divided it evenly among themselves. Within two weeks, due to personality clashes, the Marxes moved into their own apartment a few doors down. As far as I know, this was the couple's first and last experiment with communal living.

The concept of the *phalanstère* took off in North America, imported by a man named Albert Brisbane, an American who had studied with Fourier in Paris. Brisbane and his associates helped orchestrate the longest running phalanx in the States: the North American Phalanx, founded in 1843 by several families who decamped from New York City to New Jersey. On a parcel of land, the families built long halls where each had their own parlor and two bedrooms. They also built livestock holdings, gardens, a school, an artificial pond, guesthouses, a daycare center, and a restaurant. The restaurant—initially a "common table" that provided food for all with a uniform menu—served meals that could be individually selected and paid for. All workers were paid a wage according to a complex system determined by the ease and appeal of the work (lowest pay for light and rewarding labor, highest for labor deemed undesirable or taxing); there was no distinction in pay according to gender. Domestic work was taken care of by groups whose jobs rotated, and who tackled everything from entertainment to agriculture.

In 1847, after visiting the North American Phalanx, a man named John Humphrey Noyes established a 200-member home in New York State. He and his followers called it the Oneida Community. Where the North American Phalanx was secular, this project had a divine purpose. Oneida believed that Jesus had already returned, and that they were helping to build Heaven on Earth. They believed that dissolving the ties of the nuclear family would encourage greater attachment to a shared faith, and so they promoted "complex marriage," wherein non-exclusive sexual relationships were formed on the basis of attraction and desire. To have a child within the community, prospective parents would plead their case to a committee tasked with selecting good matches based on the spiritual and moral qualities of the parties involved. In 1880, Oneida began manufacturing silverware and tableware, transferring their holdings to a joint-stock company called Oneida Community Limited. During both world wars of the early twentieth century, Oneida thrived by manufacturing tableware for the military and products for use on the battlefield: rifle sights, hand grenades, guns, bayonets, aircraft fuel tanks, and chemical bombs. (By now it should be clear that these are ambivalent forebears at best; at worst, morally bankrupt, depraved, randomly quite capitalist.)

In Australia, too, utopian visions unfurled across the newly colonized land. The earliest known commune in Australia was called Herrnhut. It began in 1853 in Port Phillip Bay, now known as Melbourne. The founder, a Prussian-born preacher named Krumnow, moved with about forty people to a plot of land where they built a stone church, kept sheep and cows, and practiced fervent prayer. Krumnow had bought the land with communal money but put his name on the deed; when he refused to change it, several members abandoned the group. In 1880, Krumnow died, leaving the Herrnhut community heavily in debt. It continued under new leadership, dissipating slowly, until 1897.

In South Australia in the early 1870s, reports emerged of a strange new commune based in a rural outpost:

For Discussion and Resolution

A Spinster Land Association is the latest idea out. "Such an institution is," says Eucalyptus, in the Border Watch, "established at a place called Binnum Binnum. Many rumors are afloat as to the principles of this Amazonian confederation, some maintaining that they have founded the society on pure Amazonian or Quaker principles."

Spinster = code for lesbian. Amazonian = code for lesbian. Spinster Land Association = Australia's first ever lesbian separatist commune? Save for the above, which comes from a newspaper article published at the time, I can't find any other information about this endeavor (and believe me, I've tried).

In Queensland, after the Shearers Strike of 1891 collapsed, a group of unionists—all men, this time—seceded to Western Queensland to set up their own commune farming produce and cattle, holding their earnings in a joint fund. It was known as the Alice River Commune. One newspaper at the time compared it to Oneida, and reporters—as well as politicians interested in communalism—visited often. They found the men living harmoniously in an "Eveless Eden," with a roster for cooking, a swimming hole, a library, a flourishing vineyard, and plenty of leisure time. Some thought the absence of women and children the key to their success (no idle bodies to provide for); others thought this made the commune a futile experiment, far removed from real-world conditions. Over the years, its membership declined, and with not enough men to do the work required, the farm began to struggle and its soil quality deteriorated. In 1904, it became a Limited Liability Company, its assets divided equally among members, who promptly began to sell off their shares to new members. It disbanded entirely in 1907.

At the same time as the charismatic patriarchs began their social engineering, Fourier's ideas were also being adopted by proto-feminists. In 1868, fed-up American housewife Melusina Fay Peirce developed the concept of cooperative housekeeping in a suffragette magazine called *The Revolution*. In cooperative housekeeping, a group of women would band together to pur-chase a building in which to manufacture all household goods, which are then distributed to households for cash on delivery, meaning effectively that husbands—the only members of the family bringing in wages—pay their wives for their domestic work. In cities, "every tenth block would contain the kitchen and laundry and clothing house" and individual houses would be built without these amenities. Peirce's plans were motivated by a desire to increase the standing of women in the family and in society. And, though she writes that former servants and employees would work side by side, this was more to increase the efficiency of the household than to abolish class divisions; the co-ops would dispense with the need for what she saw as lazy and costly domestic help. Her ideas were taken up in later decades by housing reformists in New York, who built apart-ment blocks and tenement houses with common spaces and facilities.

In 1848, a suffragette named Jane Sophia Appleton pub-lished *Vision of Bangor in the Twentieth Century*, a speculative fiction imagining Bangor, Appleton's hometown in Maine, 130 years in the future, in 1978. She adapts Fourier's ideas for an urban setting, and puts them to work in service of women. The city would have communal "eating houses," covered arcades, shared amenities for tenants in blocks, higher taxes for the rich, and co-ops for the poor to buy their food and supplies at cheaper cost; women would be paid wages for their work. The narrator explains the society to a time traveler from the Victorian era:

> Just think of the absurdity of one hundred housekeepers, every Saturday morning, striving to enlighten one hundred girls in the process of making pies for one hundred little ovens! (Some of these remain to this day, to the great glee of antiquarians.) What fatigue! What vexation! Why, ten of our cooks, in the turning of a few cranks, and an hour or so of placing materials, produce enough pies to supply the whole of this city...

By the early 1900s, Appleton's vision was in danger of being supplanted by new technology, and new government policies. Objects that were once built into houses and apartments — stoves, ducted vacuum units, complicated refrigeration systems — began to be redeveloped as portable commodities for individual use. Thousands of single family homes were built in the suburbs — empty boxes that had to be filled with amenities from scratch. Home economists advocated for women as housekeepers, contributing to the economy by consuming while their husbands produced. This only applied to wealthier women, of course, and poor women ran households while earning a living as well.

Still, Appleton certainly got the decade right. In 1970, Shulamith Firestone published *The Dialectic of Sex: The Case for Feminist Revolution*. I'd say that Firestone goes harder than Fourier, harder than Appleton, harder than just about anyone, and while it's a text, not a commune, its spirit animates the many real-world experiments that followed in the '70s. (When I first read Firestone amid a stack of contemporary poly books, I thought, *Ok*, this *is something I can get behind*.)

In *Dialectic*, Firestone dreams of a polymorphously perverse society where gender disappears; she argues that marriage feeds off sex work, not vice versa; that children are oppressed; that biology is as mutable as ideas ("pregnancy is barbaric," she writes, better outsourced to artificial wombs). Her argument is simple: the biological nuclear family must be abolished. She suggests, in its place, an arrangement called "households": groups of seven to ten people — two-thirds adults, one-third children — living together for a self-determined but defined amount of time, with domestic work and childcare distributed equally. She argues that with "the wise use of machines, people could be freed from toil, work divorced from wages." To supplement this "cybernation," and to ensure women and children's freedom from men, every member would receive a guaranteed basic income.

In 1971, a group of men and women moved from Greenwich Village in New York to Haight-Ashbury in San Francisco to form the Kerista Commune. Its genesis was earlier, in the late 1950s, when an ex–air force officer named John Presmont began to hear voices telling him he would found the next great religion. He amassed followers over the next decade, who joined him in a series of loose, hedonistic experiments, before finding suitable housing in Haight-Ashbury. During the 1970s, Kerista's numbers fluctuated, with a temporary high of thirty members in 1978 living across half a dozen rented flats.

I'm not sure if the Keristans ever read Firestone, but their blueprints for sex and relationships are strikingly similar.

For Discussion and Resolution

Kerista was built around "The Utopian Social Contract of Kerista Village," a charter of twenty-six standards for living in the village that took over five years to draft and agree on. The first standard is an intention to a lifetime involvement with the village; the second is "Orthodox Polyfidelity." Kerista was composed of kinship groups called "Best Friend Identity Clusters" (B-FIC) of up to nine men and nine women. The members were polyfidelitous to their B-FIC; they did not have sexual contact outside their cluster, used a rotational sleeping roster to strengthen one-on-one ties equilaterally, collectively managed finances, and cared for any children communally. On joining Kerista, new members would enter into discussions with a potential B-FIC; if all members agreed, they were accepted. If not, they remained unattached while seeking a more suitable cluster.

In 1986, a woman named Sun joined the commune, bringing with her a Macintosh computer. Kerista used it to draw up sleeping schedules, perhaps forging the (now iron) link between scheduling technologies and poly-management. In the late 1980s, Kerista opened a Mac rental store called Utopian Technology. Soon after, Apple granted Kerista a dealer's license, and the business was incorporated in the names of four women as Abacus Inc. This was a flex of proto-Lean-In business nous; as the only female-run licensed Apple resellers at the time, they were able to win contracts with companies who wanted to look progressive. Kerista's current-day website describes Abacus as a "moderately successful microcomputer reseller." An article in *Wired* from 2002 states that at its height Abacus employed 125 people and generated $35 million in sales. (It is unclear whether or not this profit was subject to the charter determining collective finance.)

Despite the success of the business, in archived emails and accounts of this time, there are veiled references to trouble brewing, hints that the founder, now going by the name of Brother Jud, acted outside the standards while imposing them on others, rumors of bullying and coercion—a sick woman was denied her request for treatment, Abacus employees were forced to work twelve-hour days. In 1991, the commune expelled Jud, and in the same year, the tech market was flooded with computers, causing prices to plummet and leaving Abacus with a cache of useless stock. The commune disbanded, and in 1992 Abacus merged with the IT consultancy company Ciber. Kerista's main legacy is the term "compersion," a word coined with a ouija board after two members realized there were no existing terms for their positive feelings about sharing partners. Compersion is the opposite of jealousy—happiness for your partner's romantic success—and is still a buzzword in poly communities today.

Some 70 kilometers from Haight-Ashbury, members of the neo-pagan religious group the Church of All Worlds were conducting their own experiments in communal living. Throughout the 1970s and '80s, Morning Glory Zell-Ravenheart—neo-pagan community leader, witch, and priestess of the Church of All Worlds—lived on a ranch in Mendocino County with her husband Oberon and close to one hundred other families. There was a free flow of sex and love throughout the commune, and Morning Glory and Oberon had many lovers, both casual and long-term. In a 1990 article, Morning Glory termed their relationship style as "poly-amorous," minting centuries of diverse, culturally specific practices into a currency that would circulate primarily in the white liberal Anglosphere. In 1992, the Australian chapter of the Church of All Worlds was founded by

Fiona Judge and Anthorr Nomchong, and legally incorporated in November that year. It is still active, headquartered just outside Brisbane, Queensland, though polyamory is now less central to its belief system. As their website tactfully puts it, today "we each make our own choices regarding our relationships and relations with others."

In 1997, Dossie Easton and Janet Hardy, two Californians active in the kink scene, coauthored *The Ethical Slut*, opening the floodgates for a whole subgenre of self-help: poly how-to manuals. *The Ethical Slut* contains a loose history of poly and some anti-capitalist speculation on poly's possibilities, which, in the subsequent texts it inspired, would be written out in favor of hard-headed pragmatism. It remains one of the definitive guides to ethical non-monogamy. (Kim Tallbear, a theorist who writes on indigeneity and polyamory, points out that "ethical non-monogamy" implies monogamy is ethical in the first place.)

Also in 1997, Greg Araki released the film *Nowhere*, which features a bisexual polyamorous trio. Mel, the point in the open V (an arrangement where one person has two partners, but those partners aren't dating), consoles her doubting lover with as good a definition of polyamory as any: "You know that I firmly believe that human beings are built for sex and for love. And that we should dole out as much of both as possible... And just because I make it with other guys and girls, it has no effect whatsoever on my feelings for you..."

In 2006, "polyamory, -ous, and -ist" were added to the *Oxford English Dictionary*, with Morning Glory credited for the term.

In 2009, aged nineteen, I moved from a small town named Maryborough, in Queensland, to Brisbane, where I met my first "poly people." B was six or seven years older than me, a philosophy student who showed up to parties in a dressing gown and who had waist-length, religious-seeming hair. When I met her she was dating several people including L, another philosophy student, a casualty of Stanley's box wine and the French cinema class we all took. L wore only black, had yellow fingers from rolling cigarettes, and was dating both a literature student and the literature student's right-wing politics professor.

In 2014, poly partners Franklin Veaux and Eve Rickert published *More Than Two*. In opposition to gentler texts like *The Ethical Slut*, *More Than Two* targets mono-normativity in all of its forms, arguing that non-monogamous relationships can only be truly ethical if non-hierarchical: if partner A is equal to partner B is equal to partner C.

In 2015, news emerged of "The Fabulus of Unicorns," a London-based polyamorous group whose members identify as unicorns. Unicorns are a kind of short circuit in poly's history. In the 1980s, Morning Glory and Oberon "discovered" unicorns by surgically manipulating the horn buds of baby goats to grow from the center of their heads. In contemporary poly-speak, unicorn refers to the rare and highly sought supplement to a poly couple: someone (usually a woman) who wants to have sex with or date both partners.

In 2015, unaware of any of the history that precedes this decision, I opened my relationship with J. We grappled both with the hundred petty indignities it invited into our lives (suddenly, his phone has a password) and with a monstrous hitherto unrevealed capacity for insecurity, jealousy, and emotional miserliness, all concealed beneath the immaculate trompe l'oeil of our Tinder profiles.

For Discussion and Resolution

In 2017, I moved to Melbourne without J where, in the rarefied circles of the queer youngish inner north, everyone's relationships are poly, open, or, at least, caveated.

*

In the popular imagination, polyamory never really loses its roots. Its public image is inextricable from the specific strain of geek culture that communes like the Church of All Worlds and Kerista helped inaugurate. Now, on OKCupid profiles and in Tinder bios, "queer, geeky, poly, kinky" appear together so often they are practically idiomatic. This iteration of poly is stubbornly alien to both the nouvelle vague image of non-monogamy—*Jules et Jim* by Truffaut—and the Hollywood version forwarded by films like *Vicky Cristina Barcelona* and *The Dreamers*. It has an embarrassingly utopic bent borne of science fiction and fantasy (the Church of All Worlds is based on a religion from Robert Heinlein's *Stranger in a Strange Land*), though somewhat deflated by the terrestrial pragmatism of scheduling and painstaking communication.

Polyamory's lamentable sensibility stems from its exclusivity—ironically, an exclusivity that no one particularly wants to join. It's not for nothing that poly's current-day avatar is a white neckbeard huffing crumbs across his keyboard as he posts on r/relationships. Polyamory, as one common critique goes, is made possible by a life of relative structural ease. You need the time and energy to do it; you need support systems, which usually form within progressive urban centers; you need access to contraception and health care; you need a decent-paying job, or a financial safety net, to facilitate all of the above.

Note here that I'm talking about polyamory, not related forms — among them, relationship anarchy and what Angela Willey, a scholar of non/monogamies, calls "dyke ethics" — that attempt to divest from both monogamy *and* polyamory. Polyamory is thought of as a practice, sometimes an orientation, and, increasingly, an identity and a subculture. A one-off kiss with someone other than your partner but with your partner's consent does not make you polyamorous; the scaffolding that allows the kiss to happen, on the other hand, gestures toward a polyamorous ethos. Promiscuous coupled queers, especially gay men, are rarely seen as polyamorous and are perhaps less likely to identify as such; non-monogamy from gay men is viewed as natural, or at least natural to gay culture, dispensing with the need for a separate moniker. In any case, many poly people don't want their own nuanced forms of non-monogamy tarred with the same brush, so polyamory is more and more taking on an identity of its own.

There are four main negative responses to polyamory from monogamous-leaning people:

1. Ridicule and hilarity. An emphasis on its geekiness. This is often performed by otherwise progressive young lefties who give themselves a free pass to make fun of, or dismiss, poly. See: *Vice* magazine. See: conflation of aesthetic and moral objections. See: Twitter.

2. The "objective interest" response. See: endless online articles about "what is polyamory?," features on

polyamorous individuals, couples, and groups. See also: Tilda Swinton.

3. Suspicion and hostility: thinly veiled take-downs framed as "investigations" into polyamorous lifestyles. See: "polyamory wouldn't work for me"; "polyamory doesn't work"; "I'd like to be poly but I'm too jealous." See also: legitimate critiques of uneven power dynamics. See also: the Franklin Veaux debacle — the hard-line author of *More Than Two* who has recently been accused of decades of abuse by his co-author Eve Rickert, and several other women.

4. Absolute outrage. Moral panic. Decline-of-Western-civilization discourse.

In response to these, polyamorists are tasked with defending their relationships; in interviews and essays, poly people emphasize the bigness of their love, the richness of connections, their personal growth. There's always a question about jealousy to which the poly person submits the standard response: "Of course I still get jealous. But when I do I work through it."

Whatever the angle, polyamory is rarely discussed beyond the confines of empowerment for individuals, couples, and — at most — small units. As long as polyamory remains sequestered in a hero's journey narratives of personal triumphs over jealousy, insecurity, and possessiveness, over the limitations of monogamy to sexual and emotional freedom — as long as this remains the end point of the poly unit — its political potential remains obscured. As long as poly is only ever discussed according to whether or not it "works" — when its end goal becomes the cohesiveness and harmony of the unit, when it is constantly asked to defend itself — it is framed as an aberration, requiring polyamorists to spruik its benefits, reiterating the narrative of triumphs over jealousy, insecurity, possessiveness. And as long as polyamory is subject to an overemphasis on its unorthodox sexual customs, polyamorists will define polyamory not only in opposition to monogamy but to promiscuity, polygamy, infidelity, free love, and swinging: a sanitized, secular, moral, and implicitly hetero form of love — emphasis on the love, which is used to sell a suspicious mainstream on all manner of forms (gay marriage being the most obvious example). Within this closed loop, the highest achievement for poly is banality.

Polyamory becomes what Angela Willey calls a "minoritizing discourse." This is a kind of ecological approach to relationship forms that does not seek to displace monogamy but to position polyamory as something that can flourish harmlessly alongside it. Again, gay marriage is a good example: *if you don't like gay marriage, don't get gay-married.* Of course, as things stand, this means that monogamy remains at the center, polyamory at the margins — in a structurally monogamous society, the forms will never have true equality. You can see how this plays out in an influential study of "monogamous" prairie voles. Led by neurobiologist Dr. Willem Young in the early 2010s, the study claimed to have isolated hormones and even a gene determining the tendency toward commitment-phobia (vasopressin and RS3 334, a section of the gene coding for vasopressin receptors, if you wanted to know). The study and the hyperbolic media coverage it generated framed non-monogamy as a pathology to be fixed with scientific intervention—for example, straying partners could take oxytocin, the so-called bonding hormone, in pill form.

The counter-strategy, a "universal" approach, might read the above results and reverse the terms; if there *is* such a thing as a cheating gene, perhaps non-monogamy is natural and monogamy the aberration. Universalists could cite the percentage of non-monogamous species in the animal kingdom ("only 3–5% of mammal species mate for life"), or conjure primitivist tropes of polymorphous perversity before European invasion, or reference broken homes, or Ashley Madison, or the divorce rate—is anyone *actually* monogamous?

In both approaches, it becomes a matter of bringing human nature and social structures into harmony. Non-monogamy can be fixed or prohibited in order to meet the ideal of a monogamous society. For polyamorists, society can be overhauled to match the non-monogamous reality we already live but strenuously deny. In each case, the apparent naturalness of a tendency, whether it's toward monogamy or non-monogamy, remains unquestioned. It's always possible, of course, that both monogamy and polyamory are deeply unnatural.

*

A friend goes to a poly meetup.

"What was it like?" I ask.

"It was like standing in a room of people I wanted nothing to do with."

People Who Lunch

J and I try for a hierarchical poly. We are each other's primary partners. We will devote most time and energy to each other. Our setup will act to preserve the relationship; we don't want to let desire for others get in the way or shorten what will be, we are sure, the longest relationship of our lives. Other people will be secondary to this (we get this terminology — "primary," "secondary" — from 2008's *Opening Up* by Tristan Taormino, a guide for couples transitioning to non-monogamy). Weekends are ours, as are family events. We introduce subtle distinctions. Neither of us will have veto power over the other's potential partners or hookups, but we expect that we will each act carefully, taking into account the other's feelings before leaping into something new. By the time we would even get into a situation where we had to make such a choice, we would already know the other's feelings because of our comprehensive practice of communication. No conflict could arise that had not already been scheduled — preemptively, in the normal run of business — for discussion and resolution.

We open up on a Monday. J has a date on Wednesday. They start seeing each other immediately — going on dates, sleeping over at each other's houses. We had not discussed this. She is known to me; our friendship groups have recently begun to merge. Her name is L. She is like a beautiful troll: short and broad-faced, she walks with a rolling stomp. In conversation, she listens so hard she pouts, and nods in a way that looks as though she is ducking. She has pore-less, tanned skin, honey-brown hair, big cheekbones. Her face has nominated her lips to be its envoy; they lead into the world even ahead of her nose. When she laughs or smiles, dimples drill into her cheeks. She is also kind, and thoughtful — not the nemesis I wanted her to be.

On Thursday night, I go to J's house wearing the sloppiest

clothes I can find. I think: *I am going to be the ugliest bitch you've ever seen. I am going to be the anti-L.* I am wearing a long skirt with holes that a rat chewed in it and an enormous black T-shirt with a picture of Shania Twain on the front. He doesn't even notice. He kisses me with lust.

Two months in, we have a meeting on the grass outside the State Library. L wants to see J more. J is stuck, having to placate both of us; he does want to see L more, of course, but our relationship needs four nights a week (four nights is what we decided on at the start, which, as I write this now, seems totally insane). She has to believe him; the inequity in time doesn't mean an inequity of affection. We can only appeal to tradition: the vintage of our relationship, its preexisting needs. L decides to end things with J.

I take a walk by the river, eat an apple, go into the library to pee, browse the shelves, waiting for J to call. He doesn't. I walk back to our spot. J is there alone.

"What happened?" I ask.

"We decided not to end it."

Pretty soon after, they are in love. He picks me up from the movies to tell me. I haven't been expecting to see him—he had gone over to L's deal with a crisis. I watch my friends walk back into the cinema to see the next movie. Facing me from the driver's seat, he takes both of my hands and tells me. I notice that his hair is damp, that he smells like soap.

"Did you fuck?" I ask, "then come straight here to tell me?"

He is stung. It's New Year's Day and buses are down. A tiny part of me realizes I need him for a ride.

I discover too late that what I actually want, had wanted all along, is not polyamory but an open relationship: something opportunistic and frivolous and anonymous. J had wanted polyamory, had been doing polyamory, and was, annoyingly, within the letter of our agreement. I cry for days.

My best friend, E, is calm, smoking a cigarette on the veranda. She ashes into a pot plant and dog-ears her book before turning to advise me.

"It makes sense they're in love. Why wouldn't they be? That's normal. What's weird is the way they turned it into an event. Coming to see you? Why bother? It's juvenile."

I can see her critique of the situation tugging at the edge of her dislike for J.

"It makes sense you're upset. You've been socialized to see other women as the end of the world. He can't understand that."

I feel a kind of pleasurable intensity I have never felt before, or, the pleasurable intensity makes me feel something I have never felt before, which I take to be heartbreak. To hurt them back, I regard their love with the icy skepticism of a philosopher working out logical proofs. I send extremely formal text messages. I tell them I don't believe they are in love. I try to convince them of it. (Now, more than three years later, I don't believe in love at all, at least not the kind that announces itself as an event, an unknowable mystery. Saying "I love you" or "I'm in love with you" is like throwing a ball at someone's back and yelling "catch!")

Franklin Veaux and Eve Rickert, the polyamorous now-ex-couple-authors of *More Than Two*, who I resent for their hard-line attitudes and not a little in bad faith for their embodiment of every humiliating poly stereotype, calls this event — the person who walks into a rule-bound poly setup and disrupts its operation — the "game changer." Hopefully, they advise, it will catalyze the dissolution of the hierarchy, which is often an attempt to control the secondary's relationship with a primary partner and is therefore inherently unethical. And if the preexisting partners can let go of the hierarchy, their relationship will benefit too. No longer making decisions out of fear — of being replaced, of losing a unique connection — they will experience a more authentic form of love.

The experts often treat poly as a process of purification. It's a little bit Christian: through trial and tribulation and steadfast faith, you will find the core of what matters — Jesus/love. But as you strip back a relationship, the love that supposedly underpins it can become ever more elusive, more obviously bound up in pragmatic considerations — time, circumstances, rituals — and the relationship can begin to resemble related forms that we don't necessarily associate with love: friendship, dating, casual sexual arrangements, even a collegial project. Love does not preexist the forms into which it is cast; the form itself changes the love. Polyamory is the practice of learning that love doesn't exist *qua* love; it dissolves its own premise and, at the same time, reifies the pursuit of love.

Far from purifying our love, the division of our relationship into component parts has allowed a ruthless logic of quantification to flourish. I can now calculate precisely the amount of jealousy it is reasonable to feel. I am like one of Kafka's bureaucrats, rational to an irrational system, fastidious within its absurdities.

*

Before we open our relationship, we play at live-in monogamy. J has a wealthy coworker, a tall man in colorful socks and soft leather shoes. He and his wife and child are visiting the States. He needs housesitters to feed the cats and to keep them from going outside. We agree to spend a month there.

The house is a tall Queenslander on a leafy street in West End. The house has been raised and stands higher than its neighbors; inside, I never lose the sense of being ungrounded, held aloft. It takes three keys to enter through the front: one for the veranda door, one for the wooden front door, one for the mesh security door behind it. Inside, there is a bookshelf stuffed with NPR-issue novels, framed promo posters for *This American Life*, Aesop soap dispensers, a real Eames chair, a marble kitchen countertop with $100 on it for "supplies," which we immediately spend on pizza. The grass in the backyard is not the kind you can sit on. The cleaner, J's coworker informs us, will continue to come weekly while they are away.

During our first days alone in the house, we try to relax and enjoy our sudden windfall. But the house, so lively during our visit — the toddler shooting wheeled toys across the floor, J's coworker demonstrating the clarity of his speaker system's bass, his wife polishing wineglasses — settles around us. We spread out as much as possible and still occupy only a tiny amount of space, our belongings—my books, J's music stuff—pathetically scattered across the vast upcycled dining table. The house is outfitted like a spaceship, fully organized with supplies for the nuclear unit, synced to their devices and rhythms—it seems to know we are impostors and refuses to calibrate.

In the cupboard there is a maroon mug with a portrait of Trotsky on it. I take to drinking my morning coffee from it on the top floor's back balcony. We are sleeping and bathing on the bottom floor of the house, the granny flat, but we spend most of our time up here. My own sharehouse has a tiny, fully enclosed veranda, an iron cage stuffed with plants and water-warped chairs, and the rest of the house is, in any case, half outside, wind slicing through floorboards and walls of windows, doors always open, walk down steps onto grass. Getting to the backyard from this house requires dedication: making sure the front entrances are locked, going down to the first floor (there is no access to the backyard from the second floor or from the front, except through a locked gate), sliding open heavy doors with complicated latching systems, sliding them shut to keep the cats in without locking yourself out.

I'm drinking coffee from the Trotsky mug and reading. J is vacuuming the floor naked—we've spilled oats. This house doesn't feel like a domestic sphere, warm and restorative. Not that feelings on this matter matter. So, a calculation: the kitchen and all of its appliances cost, what? Twenty grand? Thirty? Forty? We are living the paid invoice of a gift registry. We are living Lillian Gilbreth's kitchen work triangle, her now-ubiquitous design of kitchens arranging stove, fridge, and sink at harmonious distances, points on a triangle, to cut down on wasted steps (the kitchen as an open V). We are living the success of Christine Frederick's vision for a Taylorist home economics. We are living thousands of tiny innovations whose sources I don't know — the insinkerator, the pantry light, the soft-close drawer runner — all of which have been patented, manufactured, shipped, bought, sold, bought, assembled, installed, and can be replaced by new versions of the same products. We are living an automation of labor that somehow still creates enough labor to employ a weekly cleaner, who is from Malaysia, and a woman. It is not so much a site of leisure as the hypothesis of future leisure. Leisure is whatever is necessary to restore the worker to the full capacity required by their work. For J's coworker, the house is wanton with its offerings; whatever it unleashes will be reabsorbed into the production process. For us, menially employed, it withdraws, meting out only necessities. (We go the whole month without finding the air-conditioning control panel.)

Even so: the dryer, the cleaner, the dishwasher, the water pressure in the shower, the ice-maker in the front panel of the fridge, the tubs of premade muesli. We are sodden with latent productivity. We don't know what to do with ourselves. We are both working a few days a week and trying to write and make music. We are both working a few days a week and not managing to write or make music. We start having fights about chores, who's not doing them and who is, and about each other's declining mental health: who is or isn't making it the other person's problem. A possum strolls through an open window and won't leave for hours. The cats escape to the garage and won't come up, streaking through towers of wine cartons, headbutting the small diamonds of night air in the lattice. Our friends come over for dinner and we finally figure out how to play our own music on their system. They leave and I'm the one to clear the plates, stack the dishwasher, wipe the table, J staring dead-eyed into Ableton. When, at the end of the month, we return to our separate houses, we decide to open up.

*

If monogamy, especially in wedlock, was once the most efficient means of accumulating capital, it does not necessarily follow that polyamory is anti-capitalist. Here's one story, or perhaps the same story told otherwise: smug poly units as mini-corporations, privatized, mobile stores of human capital. With one or two breadwinners and 2.5 kids, accumulation is capped, dispersed, rerouted. With several breadwinners, the poly unit presents a marked economic advantage. Given extra attention, parental love and financial support times two or three, the children of poly units get ahead at school and university, growing up to enter their own strategic alliances, alloys of love and money: no need to choose between material and emotional wealth when you can have partners providing both. The nuclear family transmits wealth generationally, depositing centuries of accreted fortune in the laps of its heirs. In the poly unit, the accumulation of wealth and privilege need not take centuries; it can happen in a single generation.

Polyamorous parents have an edge in the workplace; their relationships and family units have enough flexibility to take brutal hours and overwork in their stride. One parent might travel for work; the other might care for the child; the other might hold down a hospo job. There's no need to advocate for parental leave, or for the state to provide it, if there are two other parents able to pick up the slack.

In this story, artificial or ectogenetic reproduction—synthetic wombs capable of bringing an embryo to full term—is developed, trialed with genetic material stolen from prisoners and refugees. Corporations rush to patent the technology. This enacts a mass redundancy on the "world's back womb," the surrogate mothers largely situated in the Global South, who previously carried children for Western parents unable or disinclined to do so themselves. The poly unit prefers the "clean" gestation of an artificial womb rather than the polluting effects of another's body. This way, they avoid the risks of bodily pregnancy, including the power it affords the surrogate (or member of their unit) over the product of their labor—by threatening to keep the child, to "strike" by threatening to abort, or to refuse abortion at the paying parent's demand.

The death of the "natural instinct" for childbirth constitutes a new market. At first, as in surrogacy, only the wealthy or those willing to accrue huge debt can afford it. The poor undergo the retrogressive version of conception and pregnancy by trial and error, while for the rich it's business as usual until the baby is ready. Where biological pregnancy at least presents a hiccup in the function of the labor market, artificial reproduction offers unhindered exploitation of subjects whose fertility might otherwise have rendered them unreliable or unavailable as waged workers. This results in a larger reserve of labor power, increasing competition for jobs, and decreasing workers' ability to bargain for better pay and conditions. We see a return of the wet nurse—poor, single parents whose physical pregnancies disrupt their flexibility as workers and their earning potential, and whose breast milk is liquid capital so long as the nouveau Earth-mother wants to invest.

As for the child, it is subject to the ego investments of multiple parents rather than one or two. Perhaps it has been designed as the return on these investments, spawned from multiple adult cells like Dolly the sheep, a limited-liability arrangement where each parent's financial outlay is reflected in their precise share in the gene pool—daddy's eyes because he paid a premium—and their precise share of the risk. From the start, the child is adept at moving between commitments. They no longer sell their labor but mine their human capital; in the same way that TV coached a generation of children for sedentary office jobs as adults, the child is prepped for a flexible work life, the two words—work and life—colliding once and for all (it doesn't make sense to speak of balance when there are no longer two extremes).

"Feminization" is not just a term for what happens to work under precarity; it now describes a physical process. In the West, falling sperm count due to massive environmental upheaval, smoking, stress, plastics, hormones in the waterways—no one knows exactly why yet, and so hard is it to believe, even the most dispassionate articles have the tenor of conspiracy about them—creates a scarcity that compounds privilege. As sperm banks begin to empty, the cost of buying sperm skyrockets. Polyamory, or some form of non-monogamy, becomes a necessity; coupled monogamous heterosexuality is a nostalgic indulgence.

In fact, human extinction, which has long been associated with queerness as a stopper to childbearing, sometimes claimed by queers as an affirmative nihilism, is now a problem for the straight population, for everyone. Humans' interest in having sex at all declines—report after report claims that millennials are having less sex than their parents' generation, the percentage of *sōshoku-kei danshi* is growing (these are so-called herbivore men, a Japanese coinage for the growing population of young men without much interest in sex), and a new insult, "soy boys," is leveled at effete men who have supposedly been glutted on the estrogen in food and water supplies. Meanwhile, though the population begins to fall in the Anglophone West, sparking nationalist panic over white extinction, it's not enough to slow species extinctions, climate change, heat death, the end of the world as we know it.

Heterosexuality is forced to navigate the same channels of IVF, surrogacy, and artificial insemination that were previously relegated to the pathologized: same-sex partners, trans people, the hysterectomied, single would-be parents, all those unable to reproduce "naturally." Polyamory is not just a romantic or sexual proclivity, and not just a private alliance, but the dissemination of reproductive labor into a technocapitalist infrastructure (IVF, surrogacy, artificial insemination, and ectogenesis being forms of polyamory, after all).

Incels, "involuntarily celibate," imagine a surplus of sex expropriated and denied them, a withheld wage they are owed by women. Much like precarity, involuntary celibacy has been viewed as a feminizing force. I'm not couching this in Marxist terms incidentally. This link between sex and economics informs the incel community who, as Angela Nagle argues, appropriate a traditionally left language of proletariat revolution, perhaps best illustrated by the economist Robin Hansen's sympathetic reading of Elliot Rodger's motivation for killing seven people, and attempting to kill many more, at Isla Vista, California, in 2014:

> One might plausibly argue that those with much less access to sex suffer to a similar degree as those with low income, and might similarly hope to gain from organizing around this identity, to lobby for redistribution along this axis and to at least implicitly threaten violence if their demands are not met.

If it doesn't already, it will soon make sense to speak of a left polyamory and a right polyamory. A movement whose prime insult is "cuck" obviously still wants women's fidelity to one male partner, obviously still believes in property and masculinity—masculinity as the ability to acquire and keep property, property as the safeguard of masculinity. Still, there are surely polyamorists who identify as alt-right or conservative, and there are uneasy resonances between the communities, just as there are alt-right personalities like Blaire White and Milo Yiannopoulos whose transness and queerness, respectively, do not impede their conservativism. Right polyamory materializes in the form of communes whose male leaders have unhindered access to sex with women, with whoever they want. This would not be a right recuperation of a left practice, but a continuation of the persistent thread of violence in polyamorous and communal histories.

In this future, polyamory emerges as a reaction to human-induced-climate-induced extinction but remains coupled with all the accelerating networks of exploitation, extraction, and imperialism that got us here in the first place. In this future, which looks much like the present, polyamory is a stopgap solution for individuals and small groups, for consolidating resources: a wall of care or necessity erected against a punishing outside.

*

I am newly terrified by the threat of sexual stagnation. If J and I don't have sex, it must be because he's already had it, too much of it. Polyamory makes obvious the sexual entitlement that passes generally unremarked in monogamous sexual relationships and had passed unremarked in ours. This does not mean that we are less possessive, and it doesn't translate into action or change; it just means that now we talk about it. In the guise of "communication," we worry over each new issue until it becomes so big it necessitates even more "communication." "Communication" is addictive, and our addiction to it holds open the relationship months after it should have closed.

We are not having enough sex. From Emma Goldman to Shulamith Firestone to *The Ethical Slut*, sexual freedom, particularly for women and queers, has been part of non-monogamy's promise, loosing people from the proprietary bonds that govern monogamy. Non-monogamy, in turn, is difficult to imagine without queerness or forms of sex associated with queerness: cruising, group sex, public sex, extramarital sex, promiscuity. (Polyamory skews so close to queerness that I know at least a few straight poly people who call themselves queer.)

We are having very little sex. Michel Foucault cautioned against viewing sex acts as the sole locus of transgression.

There might be more transgression in fidelity, affection, and care between a community of gay men than in the canonical image of two men circling each other in a dark street. Queer relationships make forms where there are very few available, at least in 1981 when Foucault gave the interview where these ideas appear ("Friendship as a Way of Life" in *Gai pied*). He might think differently now that same-sex marriage is legal in France, and Australia, too, or he might see this as even more reason to emphasize non-sexual, uncoupled, queer relationships. To be queer, he thought, is to create a way of life rather than to discover one's sexuality or to identify with the traits (whatever they are) of queerness. This is perhaps what Foucault means when he speaks of a "homosexual ascesis," or when he claims that the "development toward which the problem of homosexuality tends is the one of friendship."

How do you measure monogamy without sex? Sex is the fulcrum of monogamy: take it away and, conceptually, monogamy falls apart. When Angela Willey sits in on Dr. Young's lab studies of voles, she finds that the lab's definition of monogamy depends entirely on sex. First, the lab team place a male and female vole—categories that are necessarily reductive, given voles' complicated sex chromosome system and indistinguishable external genitalia—together in captivity for eighteen hours to allow them to mate; mating is meant to create a bond between the pair. Next, they place an unfamiliar female in the cage; the two females are then tied to opposite walls, and the male vole is free to move between them as he wishes. This part is filmed, and later analyzed by the lab team. If he spends more time with the "partner" vole, he is judged to be monogamous. If he spends more time with the introduced female, he is judged as non-monogamous, treated with a drug, usually oxytocin, and put through the test again.

In the eighteen hours prior to the partner test, the monogamous voles are presumed to have bonded by mating. But this part is not filmed. As Willey discovers, this is because it is not essential for the voles to have mated to form bonds — cohabitation can trigger the same release of oxytocin — and so it's not essential to know what happened in these initial hours. The lab also doesn't test for same-sex relationships. Theoretically, two female voles could pair bond, but it is impossible for two females to have sex, if sex is vaginal stimulation by a penis. And it is important for there to be a sexual component to the relationship because sex, not the voles' social habits, allows the results to translate from vole to human. As one researcher puts it, "If there's no mating involved then the link to human biology becomes difficult to understand. Are they friends? Are they partners?" (Or maybe they're "just good friends.") Willey argues that under the conditions of the test, the same confusion in categories applies to male-female bonds — how do we know if they are coupled or friends?

What the study actually tests for is social monogamy — pair bonding, with or without sex — or simply sociality vs. asociality. But sex is reinscribed in the study every step of the way. To enable the translation of results, humans are presumed to be already sexual beings. The pair-bond is presumed to be sexual in order to produce something comparable to human monogamy, which can then be studied as though it preexists the terms of the study: sex is heterosexual, heterosex makes it monogamy, and sexual dimorphism makes it heterosex. The chain continues: sexual dimorphism has long been associated with racist tropes of the primitive vs. the civilized, propagated by nineteenth-century sexologists like Richard von Krafft-Ebing; the more visually different men and women — women with less hair, men with greater bulk — the more evolved they were imagined to be.

Willey does not argue for polyamory over monogamy. Like Foucault, she looks to friendship, or what she calls a "dyke ethics" to seek forms that decenter sex as their organizing principle. Dyke relationships — if you've been in one or seen the memes, you'll know — often exist within complicated networks of exes, friends, exes-as-friends, ambiguous sexual friendships, non-sexual partnerships, non-penetrative sexual experiences, surrogates, adoption, and sperm donorship, all of which resist categorization as *either* sexual love *or* non-sexual love. They are ways of life rather than ways of having sex.

Reproduction and sex for reproduction is so fundamental to conceptions of the human that removing it opens fecund possibilities. Audre Lorde calls for a harnessing of "the erotic," a category that exceeds sexuality and becomes a kind of polymorphous perversity extended into the world beyond the human. This is grounded in the personal quotidian; for Lorde, building a bookcase, making love to a woman, and writing a poem are all experiences of the erotic. Donna Haraway sloganeers sexual reproduction's obsolescence — "Make Kin Not Babies" — and imagines a form of society in which communities make collective decisions about when to have human babies, produced between no fewer than three adults, and bonded symbiotically with a non-human species. The sym is responsible for learning about its species and with attempting to repair the conditions for its survival. Kim Tallbear writes that her deepest relationship is with the prairies, rivers, and skies of her native land.

You could say that the problem toward which polyamory tends is one of friendship—a problem because entering a poly setup usually happens for reasons of love, romance, and sex, and because polyamory impedes and reconstitutes these familiar buttresses. For this reason, the self-help books frequently talk about "relationship transitions"—particularly into friendship or non-sexual relationships—instead of breakups. As a model, friendship does not fix anything, but it begins to unfold sex, love, romance, resources, and care from their compression into couples and families.

Without sex, my relationship with J feels like a particularly chatty form of enmity, as though we are one of cinema's odd couples—Steve Martin and John Candy in *Planes, Trains, and Automobiles* perhaps—forced together by circumstances beyond our control. Instead of sex, communication gives us the velocity and sense of purpose we need; for as long as there is a problem to solve, the relationship has a future.

A phone lights up and buzzes three, four, five times. J, sleeping the crisp, clean sleep of the sober, wakes easily. Having collapsed into bed drunk at 3 a.m., I am moving through sleep like a swimmer wearing jeans. I see the light at the surface and struggle toward it. J is sitting up in bed already, nursing the phone—it was his—and thumbing it furiously. I know that the texts must be from L.

Before a party at my house: J, L, and I text for several days about how to navigate all being there in public. During the party I walk in on J and L in my room, holding hands, chatting intimately. I back out of the room, smiling in panic. After the party J and L talk about how it went. J and I talk about how it went. L and I text back and forth about how it went. She sends me a message so long that it ends in ellipses, which I click on, which then opens the full message — an iPhone feature I never knew existed — which is three times as long.

J and L have been dating for about four months when we enter a new phase of the discussion. The problem, as we see it, is that J doesn't have enough time in the week for us both. (I think now that this is like saying the problem with drowning is the color of your bathing suit.) Also, that my relationship with J has long ceased to be about anything other than J's relationship with L; that L's relationship with J was always overshadowed by my relationship with J; that we are in a throuple, with all the complications and none of the benefits. I don't know who suggested it first, but I remember the sheepish tone of voice, the shy burgeoning hope. Maybe we could all spend time together, share our relationships equally. If J spends two nights with each of us, and we all spend one night a week together, he will have two nights a week alone. (Here, I remember ignoring the warning tug in my stomach.) On our shared night we could have a sleepover, if we wanted. Would we...? We could sleep in the same bed, in a non-sexual way. (Tug in stomach, this one unidentifiable.) I would have a stake in things with L, and vice versa.

"We're all in a relationship," we say. "We are all in a relationship."

L says she'll think it over. I spend the next few days living two futures in my head: one with L, and one without. Despite the catastrophe of the last several months, I feel hopeful, wistful in advance for the loss of whichever one we discard. Then, one day, L tells J that she wants to see him, and she drives over to J's house that afternoon. She doesn't stay for long. She breaks up with him and drives home.

*

I thought the end of L and J's relationship would offer what seemed like a natural pause, an opportunity to reflect on the past few months and work on restoring our ease and trust with each other. Instead, a fortnight after the breakup, J, scrolling through Tinder beside me, shows me someone who looks cool. I've met her once before. I mutter something in the affirmative. I must have been feeling guilty — it's the only explanation. I can't bring myself to tell this story here, partly because it's too similar to the last one to be of interest. J dates her for a couple of months. I go on dates with other people. I am jealous; he is jealous. We go round and round.

The things that finally end our relationship have nothing to do with polyamory. The things that finally end it are the kinds of banal couple problems that accrue and compound over time, no matter the arrangement: vicious arguments after seeing movies together. (I don't know — for some reason seeing movies together brought out the worst in us); that we travel badly together; that I can't simulate enthusiasm when J describes episodes of the podcast he likes; that I become weird and sulky on hot days; that I want to move away from Brisbane and J wants to stay. We close the relationship after six or seven months. Another year and a half after that we break up.

We are sitting on J's front veranda. The conversation has been happening for weeks now in our bedrooms, but it's mid-morning, and sunny, and warm, and though his housemates might come out — for a cigarette, for a chat — at any moment, it feels wrong to be indoors. J lives in one of the three houses on this street that I can walk into without knocking. Between them, they share veggies, chickens, cars, cartons of beer, meals, clothes, and holidays. His neighbor, R, is dragging a borrowed lawn mower up the hill. We talk through the issues until finally, as if it's an option that has only presented itself just now, one of us says: "Maybe we should just break up." Actually, it was J who said it — I would've stalled for another week or so, hoping to wait out the growing feeling of doom. As he says it, a sense of vast confusion comes over me that begins to stretch back months and months, like the opposite of hindsight. I know, even in the moment, that a mere breakup will not stop this confusion from spreading further, backward and forward.

J goes into his room and lies on his bed, eyes open to the wall. I leave through the back door and hurry down the street, ducking my head like a papped celebrity, terrified of being seen by someone I know. I go to my own home, which is mercifully empty, and consult the chore roster. I'm on mopping the floors. The cold tap has fallen clean off and there is only a stalk pro-truding from the wall above the sink; on the soap ledge, some-one has thoughtfully placed a pair of pliers with which to grip and turn the stalk to its on and off positions.

*

Two years later in Melbourne, I'm standing in a lounge room, barefoot on the carpet, huddled to one side as three or four people dance together, drunk, mostly filming each other for Instagram rather than dancing in earnest. L isn't there but she easily could have been. We are friends now. We hang out, go to the same dinners. Sometimes when we meet up we ask each other about J. The question is always asked somewhat coyly — "do you know what he's up to these days?," "have you spoken to him at all?" — and the answer is generally "no."

Tonight, however, I am not thinking about L, or J, or J, L, and me. Instead I'm talking about D, who has fallen suddenly and violently in love with a new man. My friend E and I are struggling with indeterminate jealousies: are we jealous of their happiness, their relationship, or the ballooning of a sudden intimacy that doesn't include us? E has been crashing on D's couch and spending a lot of time with the happy couple, fielding an overflow of their love (every couple needs a third, platonic or otherwise). She says D talks about politics with a new kind of placid abstraction.

"She keeps joking about turkey basters, like how we're all gonna raise kids together. She gets to think she's being radical, but has no intention of going through with it. Meanwhile they're about to shack up together."

I tell her that I'm not sure I wouldn't do the same if someone really good came along.

"That's the thing," she says. "We all talk about it, but are we going to do it? Are we really going to do it?"

A Manifesto for Post-Work Polyamory

1. Polyamory and post-work politics have a shared history. At this precise moment, their joint future is up for grabs. This manifesto is not an attempt to marry polyamory and post-work, platonic halves re-fused, or to coax offspring from such a pairing in the manner of a young couple imagining their child as a neat amalgam of their best traits (my eyes, your skin). If anything, this is an attempt to sift through a messy and ongoing separation, which is always a way of lingering in attachment. Their joint past is steeped in intentional communities and labor unions; sexual liberation and sexual abuse; judgy self-help books and spirited Bolshevik pamphlets; microcomputing and neo-paganism; artificial wombs and fear of automation; charismatic patriarchs and communal child-rearing.

2. Polyamory is the practice of maintaining several romantic or intimate relationships with the full knowledge and consent of all parties. According to who you talk to, it is both a relationship style and an orientation, both something you do and something you are. It tends to be defined by ongoing

emotional commitments rather than sex or one-off encounters. It is relationships, of any kind, with the ceiling removed.

3. Post-work politics describes a cluster of tactics for ending humankind's dependence on waged labor for survival. Its ultimate goal is not to improve working conditions or advocate for better pay; it wants to end the regime in which labor is subordinated to the reproduction of the capitalist order. It is explicitly anti-capitalist, and advocates for a post-work society only insofar as it brings us closer to a post-capitalist one. It involves action — automating as much labor as possible, the reduction of the working week, a universal basic income (UBI) to replace the lost wage — and ideology: an anti-work ethic, and the creation of a left hegemony equal to tackling the global scale of capital.

4. Polyamory must not legitimize itself at the expense of a radical politics. Defending itself from all sides — right-wing Christian condemnation, legal impositions, smug millennial taunts, left social conservatism — polyamory often tries to banalify itself. Its legitimacy will come by putting itself on the map of a future world, not by meekly asking for territory in this one.

5. Post-work politics must not radicalize itself by re-domesticating relationships. The unequal division of labor in theorizing child-rearing, kinship, sex, and care work foists a kind of intellectual hyperemployment on those who cover these bases on top of, as a necessary part of, thinking through post-work. Its relevance will come by

recognizing its deeply feminist stakes, not by disavowing its feminist commitments and forebears.

6. Polyamory teaches us how to organize reproductive, house-hold, and emotional labor; post-work thinkers have not yet sufficiently theorized social reproduction, especially the gendering and racialization of care work. Post-work politics teaches us how to reorder working weeks and repurpose laborsaving technologies for fairer ends, and how to leverage anti-work toward anti-capitalism; polyamory is often guilty of quietly acquiescing to the techno-capitalist status quo.

7. The reorganization of labor is the reorganization of relationships; the reorganization of relationships is the reorganization of labor. But reorganizing labor may simply be a means of striking an agreement between the collective and capital — a privatization of collectivity, a strategic widening of the unit of privatization. The poly unit, or any unit, becomes a more efficient means of accumulation precisely when it becomes a more efficient means of reproducing labor power. The more streamlined one's reproductive labor, the more time one can sell, the harder one can work within this time, the more surplus value produced for capital. Post-work polyamory is an attempt to check this tendency by building anti-capitalist strategies into the ongoing practice of equitably distributing labor within relationships — that is to say, within an ever-growing collective.

8. Relationships are hard work. Post-work polyamory does not want to make them any easier; it wants to make them

everyone's problem. Relationships are only a private or inconsequential affair if you ignore the following and more: the policing of low-income families, Indigenous families, black families, and migrant families by work and welfare programs; the theft of Aboriginal children by Australian government agencies and churches; the blossoming of a domestic economy premised on replacing unpaid gendered labor in the home with outsourced, precarious labor (Uber Eats, Airtasker); pornography; the global surrogacy and reproductive industries; the ideological and techno-pharmaceutical manufacture of heterosexuality and the gender binary; the Freedman's Bureau and its enforced marriages for former slaves; Viagra and the Pill; Barack Obama's multi-million-dollar initiatives to promote the nuclear family through programs such as the National Responsible Fatherhood Clearinghouse; the family sedan; the same-sex marriage plebiscite; the smart-home collecting data on a no-longer private sphere; *The Bachelor*.

9. Post-work polyamory is not nostalgic for the Fordist family wage, in which stable employment tied people to stable, and often oppressive, relationships. It is not nostalgic for comprehensive welfare, a consistently corrupt surveillance system. Nor does it simply want to replace the family wage or welfare with a UBI, leaving recipients confined to their existing social and economic standing. Post-work is a politics of tessellation: the careful arrangement of concepts and tactics in a complementary whole.

10. Down with hippie capitalism. Both post-work politics and polyamory must decamp from Silicon Valley (down with Elon

Musk, Peter Thiel, Brock Pierce). The future of work and relationships cannot be ceded to neo-Randian capitalists or libertarians or transhumanists — or, most often, an unholy combination of the three. Post-work polyamory must cherish and privilege its connection to witchcraft, cyberfeminism, ectogenetics, cybernetic socialism, manifesto writing, utopian world-building, communal living, gay activism, anticapitalist unions, organizing workplaces, strikes.

11. Down with hippie colonial capitalism. Post-work polyamory must not simply be a gentrification of relationships, pushing out low-income earners and First Nations people in the way of Google and Facebook on the lands of the Ohlone in Northern California. It must recognize the imposition of heteropatriarchal nuclear family values by settler-colonizers on First Nations people, and take to heart the work of contemporary scholars mapping decolonial poly practices.

12. The home must cease to be source material for the efficient exploitation of workers. The contemporary office with compensations in the form of massages, snacks, and puppies delivered in Ubers is a cynical refraction of the domestic, not only of its leisure technologies but of the women and hired help who administer them. Leisure time, not just waged work, must be planned for and politicized in anti-capitalist speculations.

13. Post-work polyamory is a politics of architecture. It must extrapolate on feminist experiments in household design, remaking beds, baths, floors, and walls to reduce housework and maintenance, improve accessibility, and open unthought

possibilities for cohabitation. It is not about preserving unconditional private space as a respite from increasingly conditional public space. Nor is it about destroying respite for individuals, couples, or families. Public space itself must be a respite, not a waiting room for the private sphere.

14. Because it cuts across all other structural constraints, time is one of the largest obstacles to practicing polyamory. The best promise offered by post-work politics is the liberation of time from waged labor. In order to change the base that fosters white, economic privilege in poly communities, polyamory must ally itself with left, post-work commitments.

15. The feminist push toward acknowledging emotional, care, and sexual labor is welcome but insufficient; when did "exposure" ever pay the bills? The next step is remuneration. So-called Venmo-feminism formalizes the transactional nature of relationships, making it clear that emotional, care, and sex work are forms of work, not expressions of natural feminine tendencies. But this, too, is not enough. "Emotional labor" has become a catchall condemnation for everything from exploitation at work to, at its most extreme, giving a friend support. If anything can be labor, "labor" becomes an ahistorical category that transcends specific economic formations. And if labor becomes a private negotiation between individuals — *not my problem* — then the conditions for class-based solidarity are destroyed. Class is an outcome of a system of production, of a system of labor under capitalism, not a possession or an identity. Class is when work is everyone's problem.

Good Times in Venice

"The object of work is not to satisfy but to excite."

Paul Preciado

My friends and I take clubbing more seriously than work, dedicated in a way we can only feign to our bosses, employment agents, and jobseeker diaries. To survive dwindling prospects and dead-end casual work, we instrumentalize dedication. I don't know anyone who likes their job.

Clubbing starts long before the club. Often it begins the week before, on the first lucid day after the previous weekend. It begins by gathering informal RSVPs — "are you going to x this weekend?" — and by carving an aesthetic from infinite variables: how you will feel, what everyone else is wearing, what looks the club usually attracts and whether to swim with or against this tide, the weather, what clothes are clean, what you can borrow from friends, what you might find at secondhand shops. Where to go before the club, "what time do you want to get there?," sound clouding DJs in commutes, sourcing drugs (MDMA, MDA, ketamine, cocaine, GHB, PCP) or deciding against them. (Though drugs are an integral part of clubbing, the sober rave, far from signaling an ambivalent practice, is the pinnacle of achievement. The sober day rave — in fact, the sober morning rave — is pure dedication.) The only certainty is comfortable footwear; comfortable footwear demonstrates one's dedication to the rave.

Does one have to be dedicated *to* something, or can one just be dedicated? Dedication to clubbing is both self-discipline and the reward that would usually come after self-discipline. It is its own end, the closest you can get to dropping the *to*. In 1992, Simon Reynolds wrote that clubbing was an attempt to "cram all the intensity absent from a week of drudgery into a few hours of fervor...a quest to reach escape velocity." For the unemployed, the club is not an escape from duty but an excuse for the practice of dedication. A practice of immanence. (A Protestant party ethic?)

The day of we wake up already feeling warm ripples in the gut, a stone dropped in a pond. (Sometimes just thinking about MDMA makes me nauseous.) We do stretches in the lounge room and eat something light, listening to pop music. We drink and then at a point stop drinking. We take a tram and eye others who look like they might be going to the same place.

At the club, preparation pays off if conditions are right. Most important is a dance floor of individuals knit together fiercely, invisibly, and so without the need to be overly physically or verbally demonstrative. There should be minimal transversal movement. Each clubber should have enough room to dance. Bags should be cloaked. No phones. On the one hand it's irrational to face the front—there's usually no performance to witness—and yes, it's a little fascist in the way of the lecture theater's disciplinary architecture, in a throwback way (but that's not where twenty-first-century techno-capitalism gets you; it gets you in your 3X3cm baggie of MD, in the drop of your stomach and the dilation of blood vessels as you libidinize a stranger, in the birth control you preemptively employed for such an occasion). On the other hand, facing the front creates a sense of anonymity, blinkering individuals into a loss of inhibition that slides into a suspension of identity. We have eyes only on the back of someone else's head.

What is it to have a "good time"? What is a "good time" in the club? It's not exactly being in the moment, but a sense of being outside of time. When we work a job, we produce time along with commodities; time is not a neutral measure of productivity but is determined by productivity in the first place, the global standard of hours and minutes calibrated by waged labor. To be outside of time is to temporarily suspend the reproduction of capitalist time. To have a good time is to feel as though we are consuming time: gorging on it, luxuriating in its wastage.

When I am having a good time at the club, I feel a little behind myself, like an after-image from a flash of light. Because I am behind myself, I am also ahead; the night stretches both endlessly on and has already ended. I remember things even as they happen: kissing my friends, telling a stranger I love them, telling a friend I love them, fielding life stories in the bathroom queue. If time stays straight it can feel like walking the plank to the night's inevitable conclusion. The night's end should come as a complete surprise, concealed as it is between my own split perspectives. It ends when time re-syncs. Post-gluttony panic sets in. We gather our coats and the 7 a.m. train home is a brutal rehabituation to Western capitalist space-time: an empty container hurtling forward.

*

People Who Lunch

I arrive at the 2017 Venice Biennale on a 33°C day in late September. I am with Necho, who is living in Europe for the summer — six and a half feet of unapologetic muscle decorated by spaghetti straps and a neoprene handbag. I am slumped against their side, hiding beneath a cap pockmarked by diamantes that once spelled: ITALIA. We are sweating off sunscreen, crumpled from a sleepless eighteen-hour bus ride through Germany and Italy, staunchly Asic'd among the well-heeled patrons at the Giardini della Biennale.

"Of course the German Pavilion has a line," Necho says.

We are waiting to see Anne Imhof's performance piece *Faust*, which, among other things, riffs on Berlin's club scene, notorious for its two- or three-hour lines that often terminate in rejection. *Faust* won a Golden Lion award for best national participation and has drawn daily crowds since it opened in March. Even the durational element is reminiscent of clubbing; the performances are five hours long, six days a week, and will continue until the Biennale's close in November. It's about the cycle, the punishing accretion. Eat, sleep, rave, repeat.

"No big cameras, no flash photography, respect the performers' personal space," says the usher as we enter through the side door.

The front entrance, flanked by austere gray columns, has been blocked off with a security fence behind which are two Doberman Pinschers, languid in the heat. The pavilion, erected in 1908 but renovated in 1938 to reflect the aesthetic principles of the Third Reich, is large, high-ceilinged, and constructed from marble and cement. In comparison to other pavilions like Canada's, a graceful glass-and-wood bungalow built around a tree, it feels oppressive and immovable. Inside, the windows are positioned along the very tops of the walls, well out of view, so that light pours in top-down.

Against this weight, Imhof has somehow converted the pavilion to "Junkspace," architect Rem Koolhas's term for the disposable, fragmented buildings of postmodern public space: airports, hospitals, shopping centers. "In previous building, materiality was based on a final state that could only be modified at the expense of partial destruction," Koolhas writes, but in Junkspace, where all is modular, temporary, and easy to replace, you can tinker without leaving a mark. In 1993, artist Hans Haacke dissented from the pavilion's heritage by tearing up the marble floor of its 1938 redesign; Imhof has constructed a reinforced glass floor (or ceiling) about 1.5 meters above the restored floor. Haacke's Pavilion — entirely bare except for two wooden construction beams and the word GERMANIA emblazoned on the wall — amplified the original architecture's fascist overtones. The 2017 pavilion's fascism cannot be torn out; Junkspace is "fascism minus a dictator." Transparency — of wall, of window, of the open-plan office — offers an invitation that Junkspace's ruthless conditioning by and for the bottom line surreptitiously withdraws.

Faust's set is a continuation rather than a disruption of the analgesic design of the Biennale's grounds; the Giardini, too, is Junkspace: a miracle of suspended impermanence (chain-link fences, ticket booths, casual staff) dusted across the coagulated history of Venice. Necho and I are well practiced in navigating subtle forms of exclusion in supposedly open terrain. Unmistakably queer, as we browse the pavilions we are looked upon with a suspicion that often tips into open hostility — scoffs and glares directed largely at Necho, whose irrepressible flamboyance seems to especially offend the aristocratic ladies walking arm in arm with their linen-suited husbands. The grounds of the Giardini mandate inclusion only because we hold passes, and only for as long as our passes last.

Imhof's troupe are also visibly queer, or have at least adopted an aesthetics of queerness for the performance; they are a-gender in their gender presentation (the press release says "post-gender"), youngish, good-looking in their gauntness. Quarantined by their status as performers, their gender-fucking is a celebrated part of the work. They are dressed like Berlin club kids, which is to say like the last two years of trend reports pared down to their most pragmatic: sportswear, but not sports luxe; occasionally but not showily branded; sneakers and knee pads: more Heaven's Gate than health goth. At least one of them, Imhof's partner Eliza Douglas, models for Balenciaga.

Inside the pavilion, the performers are beneath the glass, underfoot of the audience. I watch through other people's raised iPhones. Apart from the droning music, there is a reverent hush. They crawl, slide, creep, contort, crossing paths, coupling, lingering, detangling. The performers are magnets; above the glass, the spectators are metal filings. Where they go, we go. We move without thought when the bodies are under glass, but when they move from an opening in the floor to the level of the audience, the practice of viewing is suddenly compromised. I am poured back into my body; the gaze emanates, again, from a perspective that takes up space. The bestial shapes pulled by the performers and their unexpected flights across the floor force us into an awkward improvisation. How do we cede or take ground?

I peer down and see objects scattered across the marble. A slingshot. Bowls of ball bearings. Spray cans. Water bottles. If clubbing occurs along a continuum of joy and desolation, *Faust* emphasizes the latter end, where accretion rehearses addiction and the forty-eight-hour party becomes a safety net in a vicious rental market. Towels. Charging banks for phones. Bars of soap lined up on a metal sink. A heroin kit. The lights have gone on in the club.

*

The basic drawcard of *Faust* seems to be its promise of excitement. In exhilarated tones, reviews remark on its salaciousness, citing rumors that the performers, at times, even masturbate. But why is *Faust* titillating? If you miss the masturbation scenes, as I did, what about it is sexual? Is it simply that the performers are young, good-looking, and touching each other, albeit in the manner of an awkward game of Twister? Is it that its aesthetics and postures reference BDSM? (But surely the past few years of daddy jokes and slave collars in H&M went most of the way to divorcing BDSM aesthetics from practice...?)

These references — BDSM, club culture, drug-taking, high fashion, queerness — are all decidedly amenable to the Insta-frame, and reviewers have been quick to point out its resemblance to a fashion show or commercial. Depending on where your sympathies lie, it's easy to read *Faust* as either an exploitation of or commentary on our image-obsessed culture. Implicit in both readings is the idea that art usually distinguishes itself from commerce by impeding its own value production. We like to imagine that art is produced outside of the market first, and enters it begrudgingly only when compelled to. Here, it's as though privacy fosters authentic experience, which the public world of commerce parasitically uses or encroaches on, sapping the purity of an originally non-commodified form.

Faust shows this up as a myth, one that is certainly irrelevant to a post-Fordist system of production in which the so-called public and private spheres are fully enmeshed. *Faust* is not simply an attempt to flummox the lines between art and commerce. Nor is it a cynical adherence to the "sex sells" mantra of advertising. Rather, it suggests that excitement is inextricable from production, drawing a through line from titillation to techno-capitalism. It invites us to see excitement as generative rather than simply responsive; it is an exercise in putting excitement to work.

Philosopher Paul Preciado, who is quoted in *Faust*'s press release, calls this technologically produced affect *potentia gaudendi*: the total capacity for a body's excitation. For Preciado, all labor is geared toward capitalizing on this potential. Though *potentia gaudendi* has a sexual dimension, it is not a natural wellspring of libido or desire. Rather, it is a kind of techno-vitalism, generated and sustained in the circulation of porn, medication, images, hormones, chemical compounds, money, digital signals, minerals, and genetic material of all kinds. Labor is the activation of this circulation, the "excitation-frustration-excitation" loop that remains unfulfilled, self-perpetuating. This process does not even need a living body to function; it ignores distinctions between life and death in its conversion of all life to information. "Excitation-frustration" ad infinitum: another name for titillation.

One review has it that "the dynamics of control pervade [the performer's] actions. The micro-movements demonstrate how organic beings buckle under abstract powers and systems" (Hadden Manhattan, *AQNB*). This reading poses a conflict between an already existing subject (an "organic being") and an omnipresent sociopolitical regime. Given the physical constraints of the pavilion and its planes of glass offering total surveillance, it is a tempting interpretation.

But the beings in *Faust* are not exactly controlled, nor are they organic. Rather, they are produced—self-made, even—within the technological apparatus of the work: impure, implicated, and undead, networked and dispersed as data within platform capitalism, whose avatar in *Faust* is Instagram. On Instagram, users talk into their cameras, post selfies, cultivate large and small followings, partner with brands, sell products, chat to friends, sext strangers, block unwanted attention. On Instagram, as in *Faust*, value is not extracted by force but produced in the flex of agency. Far from attempting to control or limit, it is in the interests of capital that the subject cultivates the fullness of their excitement so that it may be tapped and exploited. Under post-Fordism, the process of laboring does not terminate with its reification into an object or service. Even if one or both are produced, the production of commodities is almost besides the point. Rather, labor is the ongoing production of responsive, fluid, excitable subjects.

On the opposite side of Venice, in the Fondazione Prada pavilion, there is a video work by Alexander Kluge in which an assembly-line worker explains how she manages to stomach her job. She describes the circumscribed windows of time allotted for each task, synced to the rhythm of the machines, which permit only a limited range of movement subordinated to efficiency. She then describes how she has developed an alternate choreography within these small windows while still meeting her quotas. She whips an arm up, twirls her wrists, flexes fingers, improvises. All activity remains in service of the assembly line, but she still manages to snatch some pleasure from an otherwise crushing repetition.

Faust is the worker's alternative choreography, unloosed. The movements of the performers are ambiguous and idiosyncratic, the kinds of unproductive superfluities that were once shaved off in Fordist production but are now encouraged as productive in and of themselves. Not only do we not know what the performers will do next, we do not know what they *can* do. Despite the spatial constraints, they are unconstrained: less human than abject potential. (It does not matter whether or not the performers *actually* masturbate as part of the work, but that we can imagine them masturbating.) Within the space of the German Pavilion, we, the audience, are not just spectators and not exactly "participants." Rather, we are produced in simultaneity with the performers as subjects that are excitable, and excited-with. Call it workplace training.

In this, *Faust* is not exceptional but rather an exemplary manifestation of what Preciado calls the "pornification of labor." "The cultural industry is *porn envy*," he writes. By this he means that all forms of production increasingly mimic porn's conversion of excitement into capital; the non-pornographic arts can only dream of porn's efficiency. The difference between art and porn is that art traditionally hamstrings its own efficiency whereas porn does not. And nor does *Faust*. In this way and in this way only—not because of the performers' nudity or because its erotics transgress and transform the medium—*Faust* skews closer to porn than art.

At the club, upholding the barriers between porn and art, sex and aesthetics, is not only impossible but unprofitable. *Faust* learns from the club, removing—or making visible—the few steps separating performance and partying. It does so physically as well as conceptually, the detritus in the pavilion implying a wider context from which it has been abstracted; the performers, in their postures of dominance and submission, variously look as though teleported mid-act from a sex club, a dance floor, or a nightclub's dark room.

If *Faust* also shorthands advertising—if it looks and feels like an ad—this is because we recognize implicitly the ways in which value is generated in post-Fordism: through *potentia gaudendi*, the body's potential for excitation. In this sense, critiques that decry *Faust*'s use of reliable millennial hypemongers like Vetements-Balenciaga are justified but miss the point. *Faust* joins excitement to production within the work and, in doing so, beyond the work. The Biennale, and *Faust* within it, functions as one node in a global economy of speculation built on hype. Showing in Venice drives up the value of past and future works, and for Imhof, who also makes objects (paintings and photographs) that function as commodities, *Faust* will have been a profitable venture. A friend of a friend of one of Imhof's dancers tells me later that they quit the show in protest when they learned Imhof did not intend to pay her performers—cultural gatekeepers have the production of surplus value down to a fine art.

*

What is it to have a good time? Having a good time is so often a question of duration, of knowing when to stop. *Faust* considers what happens when you do not or cannot stop, when there is no pause available. Clubbing is not just about the rupture of stultifying repetition. Clubbing is about a knowing and voluntary capture within what you were already captured by. It's about reveling in techno's infinite escalating entrapments that feel like release but hold you fast (sometimes it's literally impossible to tear yourself away from the dance floor); in the narcosexual economy of the club toilets; in the slide from identity into a trans-personal circuit, which is less a stripping back to some raw, libidinal charge than a stripping back to the framework within which this charge thrives (a collective becoming-club, becoming-network). Clubbing happens in the *Faustian* time of Imhof's piece and of Goethe's original: a lust for perpetual pleasure, without thought for the comedown.

The difference between work and play, then, lies less in quality than in the duration of the excitation-frustration-excitation loop. Clubbing shortens it so that frustration is indistinguishable from excitation. Fordist production lengthened the loop, Monday to Friday. And if clubbing was once hostile to work and work hostile to clubbing, in post-Fordism work's BPM coincides with that of the club's. Anne Imhof's *Faust* keeps pace.

The Buffalo Club

1.

An artist and a comedian walk into a bar. It's an autumn night in London, 1822, and the weather is unusually cold for this time of year—by December, parts of the Thames will have frozen over, a once-in-a-decade event. The artist, Joseph Lisle, has curly brown hair and wears small oval spectacles. The comedian, William Sinnett, is blond and rosy cheeked. They pass the main entrance to Drury Lane Theatre on Catherine Street, turn down Russell, pass the stage door, cross the road, and enter the small, bright Harp Inn, where a large group of very drunk men greet them loudly. There are men in top hats, men carrying canes, and men wearing coats that were fashionable ten years ago, worn thin at the cuffs and elbows. An influx of actors arrive from the theater, and though Lisle and Sinnett earn their living as stagehands, they are all talking, drinking, laughing, and singing as one, all brought together under the auspices of a club called the City of Lushington.

As the name suggests, the City of Lushington is structured as a city. Its primary purpose is drinking (rumor has it that the word "lush," slang to describe an alcoholic, comes from this club). There is a mayor, a chairman, and four aldermen, who each preside over one of the four wards: Suicide, Poverty, Lunacy, and Jupiter. There are lesser officers too, including the City Taster, the City Physician, and the City Barber. The Taster's role is to taste the ale. If it is found to be delicious, which it usually is, the inn is fined two gallons. Lisle and Sinnett are untitled, part of the citizenry.

The artist and the comedian walk out of the bar. Or are kicked out of the bar. At some point, they are no longer welcome. The City is too populous and the workers — the less illustrious ones — are the first to go. The artist goes home to his garret. He has an armchair in the corner of his room under a window, a frying pan on his hearth for cooking. He is yet to publish his first book of drawings, a collection of satirical caricatures, which will come eight years later and garner him some success, but not much.

The artist and the comedian have a plan. Ousted from the City, they will start a family, albeit one without women or fathers or sons: a fraternity, only brothers, only equals. They decide to convene in the same tavern, and though it seems clear they are motivated by revenge, they claim its purpose is to "perpetuate the hitherto ignored ballad 'We'll Chase the Buffalo!'":

> Come all you wild Indians who chance to appear
> We will defend our dwellings, boys, with gun and with fear
> We will all unite together and we'll strike the fatal blow
> And we'll settle on the banks of the lovely Ohio
> We'll settle on the banks where the pleasant rivers flow,
> Through the wild woods we'll wander and we'll chase the
> buffalo.

The song was popular at the time, brought back to the motherland by English colonists in Ohio, who, by 1790, had hunted native buffalo almost to extinction. Lisle and Sinnett call their club "The Buffalo Society" and hold their first meeting at the Harp Inn in August 1822. Soon after, they become the "Loyal Order of the Buffaloes" to show their allegiance to the Parliament and Crown; gradually, through slips of the tongue lubricated by booze, this becomes "Royal." "Antediluvian," meaning "before the Flood," the biblical one, comes last, in the 1850s, as a way to add gravitas and history: the Royal Antediluvian Order of Buffaloes.

2.

By the time I learned of the Buffaloes, I had been inadvertently frequenting their Australian headquarters for years. It was a Friday night, and I was standing outside a nightclub in Melbourne called Hugs & Kisses, sometime in early 2018. I wondered aloud about the building—a two-story redbrick warehouse that looked industrial, or pre-gentrification industrial, given that "industrial" usually refers to post-industrial buildings retrofitted with industrial chic (open spaces, washed concrete, bare bulbs). The club, my friend said, was leased to a guy named Hugo by an all-male secret society who occupied the bottom floor, possibly closeted gay men, victims of an outdated repression, and definitely satanic. We were standing right outside their front door.

A few months later, I hear that Hugs is shutting down, and

that the Buffaloes have sold the building for $6.25 million. A friend of a friend puts me in touch with the Hugo in question. Hugo is Hugo Atkins, someone I've seen around — a solid mustachioed figure in glasses — but never properly met. We text back and forth, and then we speak on the phone so he can tell me what he knows about the Buffaloes. It's not much, he says, but he was initiated into their Melbourne chapter in 2010, when he was twenty-one. All up, the ceremony took about three hours over the course of a summer afternoon. He remembers arriving at their city lodge — which is also their Australian headquarters — and waiting in a vestibule dominated by a large framed painting of a buffalo, and that the men gave him "infinite ciders": "they were trying to get me wasted." He was blindfolded and led into the main hall, and he remained blindfolded for about twenty minutes as the initiation began.

"It was surreal," he says.

He remembers smoking something from a clay pipe, he remembers people chanting, he remembers the phrase "bring in the goat" — but there was no goat, it was some kind of in-joke — and receiving a password, which was kind of like a nursery rhyme where each party had to fill in the blanks. They told him secrets that he can't remember anymore, and that he wouldn't tell me if he did, and which I say I wouldn't ask him to, though I wonder whether I would be able to hold out if he were offering. At the end, he was given a "club passport" and sent on his way, swaying through the cobblestone back streets of Melbourne's city center. He had no intention of using the passport. The ritual was a formality insisted on by the old men. His own motivation was much more prosaic: property. He wanted to rent the second floor of their building, a dank warren of rooms with a long wooden bar in the largest of them, and open a nightclub there. Better still was the liquor license. The Buffaloes were officially a social club, which meant they could serve alcohol 24/7 to their members and didn't need to hire security guards or follow lock-out laws; provided that all the punters signed up ahead of entry, Hugo could throw all-night parties with impunity. And what was in it for the Buffaloes?

"There was an impending sense of doom," he says, old members dying and no new ones joining.

So they liked the club idea, at least at first, the young people coming through every week in their strange clothes, though Hugo did bend the truth and tell them it was a jazz club. Also, they needed the money. The Buffaloes owned the building, but council rates alone cost them $30,000 a year, and this plus their dwindling membership meant that they were rapidly going broke.

When you bring up Hugs & Kisses in the right company, people tend to have a lot to say. They will tell you about smoking in the tiny wedge of a room off the dance floor; about the time they saw three people fucking in one of the booths; about the time they saw someone pissing into the old broken piano that sat in the toilets next to the basins. But this, about the Buffaloes, was the most interesting thing I'd heard in a long time and I decided to do some digging.

3.

The artist and the comedian are nothing special. They are just two of the thousands of men who, at some point during Britain's industrial era, joined a fraternal club, society, or order. By the late 1700s in London — population approximately one million — there were at least 3,000 different clubs and societies. In 1778, the Freemasons had 137 lodges in London alone, 109 in the rest of England, and 171 abroad. Edinburgh had approximately 200 different societies, while in Exeter, society men could be found "boasting they have not passed one evening at home year round."

Gentlemen's clubs were second homes in the city for aristocratic and professional men in the eighteenth and nineteenth centuries, often consisting of palatial rooms with libraries, dining areas, and sitting rooms. What happened in these rooms changed from club to club and might have included: planning revolutions, playing chess, helping the needy, discussing literature, playing sports, holding debates, holding lectures and classes, advocating for the abolition or continuation of slavery, all this plus a lot of whiskey-swilling and cigar-smoking. The working-class equivalent tended to develop in industrial areas. Many of these were run by unionists, or provided a base of solidarity that could then be unionized. Yet another form of club — mutual aid and friendly societies — offered members an early form of private insurance. Members bought in and paid fees, which were paid out to members and their families for medical costs, periods of unemployment, and funeral expenses.

Then there were clubs, like the Buffaloes, that did all of the above: union-insurance-welfare hybrids, with all the benefits of a social club. They raised money mostly through membership fees and by taking donations at meetings. Unlike contemporary welfare, these societies were not universal or state-run, paying out to any who applied. They tended to form around specific trades and supported only members of the club, or their immediate families, and sometimes—more rarely—friends or strangers in need of charity. Unlike insurance agencies, they were social, not just financial. And unlike unions, most societies didn't call for strikes, or fight to improve conditions across their industry, or demand sick pay or shorter hours from their bosses; they insulated workers from the worst excesses of capitalist modernity by allowing them to shoulder the costs of their own exploitation.

4.

The artist and the comedian are minor players in a much stranger story. Around the same time they began, the early 1800s, a fervent esotericism gripped England and the Americas. Charles Dickens dabbled in mesmerism, W. B. Yeats channeled poetry from the spirit world, and the spiritualist Madame Blavatsky was followed by "raps" wherever she went. Europe plundered sacred objects from its colonies and installed them in its museums, which stoked anxieties of wrathful gods and ancient magic unleashed. The bourgeoisie and aristocracy became amateur or expert Egyptologists, Orientalists, Indophiles, anthropologists, phrenologists, eugenicists. And, alongside trade and convivial organizations, countless societies sprang up to study and practice magic.

According to one historian, Charles E. Ellis, in his 1910 book on fraternities, catchily titled *An authentic history of the*

Benevolent and protective order of Elks, the Buffalo Society was a debased offshoot of a much older tradition, one that stretches back to literally biblical times. In a section on the pre-history of the Elks, his own club (founded by an ex-Buffalo), Ellis claims that Noah, of Noah's Ark, was a Buffalo, as were King Solomon, Samson, Brutus, Marc Antony, and William Shakespeare. The founder of the Buffaloes is known only as George Cooper Murray — I've seen his name in other Buffalo lore and never been able to find anything more about him. If you believe Ellis, this is because "George Cooper Murray" is a cipher concealing his true identity to non-initiates. "Murray" revived the ancient order by establishing a lodge in London in the late 1600s, and called it "Harpocrates Lodge" after the Greek god of secrecy and silence ("Harpocrates" is the Hellenized version of the Egyptian child-god Horus the Younger). When Lisle and Sinnett started their Buffalo Society, they had the Harpocrates Lodge in mind, and wanted to revive it.

Here's where it gets complicated. Ellis won't just say it straight, but he does plant three clues as to Murray's real identity. First, he claims that the name is a *temurah*, a method of Kabbalah used to divine hidden meanings from the Bible, in which letters are rearranged to uncover latent readings. Next, that it uses *gematria*, another Kabbalistic method, in which each letter has a numeric value resulting in a unique meaning for each word and phrase. Finally, he points out that "George Cooper Murray" consists of three words, six letters each — 666, the number of the beast in the Book of Revelation.[1]

---

1. There are actually three types of temurah — *atbash*, *avgad*, and *albam* — and Ellis does not specify which method has been used here, so bear with me as I try each. First, though, you have to translate "George Cooper Murray" into Hebrew, the

To make matters weirder, this is also the moniker of Aleister Crowley, the English writer, artist, and magician known as "The Great Beast 666" and "the wickedest man in the world." Is Ellis claiming that Aleister Crowley started the Buffaloes? In some ways, it makes perfect sense. Crowley was a habitual club-starter and joiner, and a member of at least three different societies. Another conspiracy or clue, this one promoted by current-day occultists: Crowley is on the cover of the Beatles' *Sergeant Pepper's Lonely Hearts Club Band*, as is a representative of the Buffaloes, who also resembles Crowley — bald and wearing a fez. The implication is that Crowley and the Buffalo are interchangeable, one and the same. And, during a trip to Cairo, Crowley claimed that he was visited by a messenger sent by Horus, namesake of Murray's first ever Buffalo lodge, who charged him with ushering in the Eon of Horus.

---

original language of Kabbalah. In Hebrew, words often have three consonants and no vowels. "George Cooper Murray" translated tri-consonantly is ירמ רפק גרג. Deciphered using *atbash*, and then translated back into English, this becomes "regards." In *avgad*, each letter replaces the preceding one in the alphabet, so deciphering it means replacing each letter with the next: ירמ רפק גרג becomes טקל קעצ בקב, and translates to "the captain shouted to Leket" ("leket" are ears of corn). *Albam*, which replaces the first letter of the alphabet with the twelfth, the second with the thirteenth and so on, results in a phrase that translates to "weave a thread." Using gematria, the tri-consonantal version of George Cooper Murray, gives you 756. I don't speak Hebrew and have laboriously conducted this translation with the help of several online services, kind strangers on Hebrew mysticism forums, and a Christian preacher, who is fluent, and who tells me there are several ways of translating both the decrypted results and "George Cooper Murray." He also says — and DustyFeet18 from the Abrahamic Religions thread on TheosophyNexus confirms — that "George" just isn't a Hebrew name, and might actually be equivalent to "Adam" or מדא, in which case we would need to start this whole process again. Beyond some kind of obvious reference to the devil, I don't even know what I'm looking for so it's possible that I've stumbled across the answer already but don't realize it; maybe "the captain shouted to Leket" means something to you, in which case, get in touch, but for now the cipher stays ciphered.

But, whatever the coincidences, the dates don't match: Crowley was born in 1875, and Murray is supposed to have founded the Buffaloes in the late 1600s. Time hopping notwithstanding, it seems unlikely that Crowley had anything much to do with the Buffaloes. It's more likely that Ellis was a follower or fan of Crowley who wanted to rewrite his club's history to include the wickedest man in the world, giving it classier forefathers than a bunch of down-at-heel drunks. There's also the possibility that the George Cooper Murray story is pure invention, a red herring: a centuries-old joke that makes a punch line out of people like me.

5.

To my surprise, the Royal Antediluvian Order of Buffaloes (RAOB) Australia has a website. I don't hold out much hope — it looks old and unused, done in sage green and Times New Roman — but, just in case, I send a polite inquiry to an email address listed on the page. The reply comes swiftly from someone named Greg: did I want to drop by their closing party? I pitch it to my friend as an investigative turn in my writing practice. I want to know what happens behind closed doors, find out who the old building on Sutherland Street has hosted all these years.

"Where is the money going?" I ask rhetorically.

She looks at me with alarm, then amusement, then back to alarm.

"Don't go alone," she urges. "Take someone with you."

I ask my new housemate, Liv, who has just moved to Melbourne after living in Berlin for two years. Since her arrival, she has been searching unsuccessfully for work, sitting on the mattress in the middle of her otherwise empty room, and 3D modeling her ideal bedroom layout on open-source design software. She says yes.

In preparation, I conduct research by typing every configuration of "RAOB," "Buffaloes," and "The Royal Antediluvian Order of Buffaloes" into Google. On page 1 of the results, I click through real-estate articles about the sale. On page 2, I learn that in 2009, six RAOB trustees in northern England were suspended for "misappropriating funds" to the tune of £30,000. Their suspension led to mass resignations and the closure of several lodges around England. In 2015, the Grand Lodge of England was investigated for financial irregularities; approximately £100,000 had gone missing from their books. Not huge money, in the scheme of things, but something.

On page 3, I hit the forums — message boards with names like "Australian Land Rover Owners" and "Above Top Secret":

> Beacon: In a new video from Beyonce she appears to be wearing the insignia of the RAOB — The Royal Antideluvian Order of the Buffaloes — and displaying their motto, Justice, Truth, Philanthropy!

> Birdy123: I believe that raob is a very secretive group as I cannot find much information on them. Im very interested to find out more if anyone is kind enough to help. I have pictures if anyone would like to see

Buffalo67: I have read some of the posts here with mounting trepidation, and have to confess; Yes we are evil and run the World. Sorry. Yeah, right…we are a Fraternal Society i.e. no girlies (Women can join The Glades which is of course our sister organization).

On page 4, I find the video of Beyoncé; she really *is* wearing an RAOB medallion.

When the day of the party arrives, Liv and I dress carefully: a denim skirt, linen pants, two monochrome ironed T-shirts between us. We take a tram to the city and walk down Elizabeth Street in the direction of the river. Greg had said to come by some time around 1 p.m.; it's now 1:30 and I'm getting antsy. I stride forward, and Liv walks half a step behind, smoking a cigarette, an unhurried European saunter, a *dérive*, somehow seeming to move sideways rather than ahead. We speculate about the party and plan our approach. We will not lie to the Buffaloes, we agree, but we will not correct them if they happen to assume we are journalists. This isn't for any nefarious purpose but for our own self-regard. She will be the photographer; we have brought along a disposable camera. I will be the interviewer. By the time we turn down the alleyway leading to the club, it's almost 2 p.m. I feel my stomach constrict, picturing men in suits squinting at fob watches.

On Sutherland Street, which is more an alley than a street proper, there are three people smoking tailors of a particularly pungent variety and laughing uproariously. One of the people is a woman—a girlie?—with hair frazzled from years of packet dye, swigging from a bottle in a brown paper bag. The man on her right has a thin face with watery blue eyes and has raked back his few remaining strands of hair with gel, which forms a lacquer over his white skull. The other man is plump, pink, and wearing a black synthetic polo shirt. They fall silent and watch us as we walk past them to the other entrance, the one that services Hugs. The door is shut. We turn back the way we came. We stop in front of them. They look at us. We look at them. I ask for Greg. Eyeing us suspiciously, the woman leads us inside.

Only months later did it occur to me that the origin story could be fake, not just in its strange particulars — George Cooper Murray, Crowley, Satan, etc. — but as a whole. The first written record of the Buffaloes comes not from the club itself, and not from Ellis's book, but from Pierce Egan's *Life in London*, a popular serial published throughout the 1820s, which follows the adventures of three young hedonists: Tom, Jerry, and Bob Logic. Together, they traverse high society as well as its gambling dens, boxing rings, taverns and, in one episode, a Buffalo initiation ritual. Egan footnotes a potted history of the club for context: "The Buffalo Society was first established in August 1822, at the Harp Inn on Great Russell Street, opposite Drury Lane Theatre. Our founders were an eccentric young artist named Joseph Lisle and a comedian by the name of William Sinnett..."

At some point, RAOB seems to have adopted this version of its history wholesale — you will find this story repeated, word for word, in the annals of Buffalo literature. But the narrators are unreliable: Tom, Jerry, and Bob Logic are fictional characters, or to be precise, personae, examples of the popular Victorian technique of using archetypal characters to explore real-life events and places from particular perspectives (Tom represents the urbane young gentleman; Jerry, the naive country boy, visiting London from the country; and Bob Logic, the amoral London chancer). It occurs to me that Lisle and Sinnett might also be personae, avatars for the working artisan's gutsy struggle against the Drury-Lane class — that the "Buffalo Club" itself could be a personae, standing in for all of London's clubs and societies.

Lisle, verified by his cartoons, his book, and short biographies scattered across the Web, seems real; Sinnett, less so. The only mentions of a "William Sinnett" in relation to the Buffaloes occurs within histories taken from Buffalo sources taken from *Life in London*. (I gave Sinnett uncorroborated blond hair and rosy cheeks to contrast with Lisle's fact-checked dark hair and glasses.) As for the Buffaloes, if they didn't exist then, they do now, somehow moving from fiction to reality in the intervening years, the proof of which is right in front of us: a dim wooden vestibule decorated by a huge painting of a buffalo standing side-on. The woman leads us into an office where three men are sitting, two bearded, one clean-shaven, all in their fifties or sixties, all tall, even while sitting, with beer guts resting on their thighs. It's just gone 2 p.m. Introductions: Greg, Graeme, Moses, Liv, Sally.

Greg is the Grand Secretary of Victoria — 70 percent billowing yellow Hawaiian shirt, with a supple-skinned face topped by short gray hair. Graeme, the current Grand Primo of Australia, i.e., the most senior position in the country, has a delicate face and bald legs, one of which is marked by a long scar that starts somewhere under his cargo shorts and runs down his calf. I'm impressed by "Grand Primo." What does the Grand Primo do?

"Bugger all," says Greg.

Moses is an ex–Grand Primo of Victoria and of Australia. He has his arms folded across a black synthetic polo with "RAOB" embroidered in red on the breast pocket, a white beard fringing a round pink gnomic face. He is a truck driver in ordinary life. I feel his gaze and find myself stealing glances at him to check if he's still watching. He always is, and with an unsmiling expression that borders on petulance. I feel a corner of my attention tune to his mood, a back channel running calculations and surveillance. All of them, in different and tesselating ways, remind me of my dad.

Liv and I perch on wooden and leather chairs along the side of the room. The three men are sitting around a table, facing us. The room, like the vestibule, is paneled in wood that emanates golden light, though it's chipped and peeling in parts, and almost every available surface is covered in knickknacks, moldering documents, framed photographs, mugs, and generally just stuff. It couldn't look more different to upstairs, which has walls painted a tarry black that become slick with evaporating sweat on packed nights. Smell-wise, though RAOB HQ carries the same base note of trapped air and stale beer as the nightclub, it is here overlaid by tea-bag tea, wood, and an old-book smell that must come from the sheaves of paper.

Greg clears his throat. "We've got a traitor in our midst."

My chair creaks as I shift my weight. He grins, pointing at a mug decorated with the Western Bulldogs' team crest. The three men start laughing, arms bouncing over chests.

"I go for the Bulldogs," I say apologetically, trying to join in.

It's a mistake—I've only watched one AFL match ever, not featuring the Bulldogs, and the next few minutes pass in increasingly abstracted banter, petering out into silence.

"I'm from Queensland," I say. "Originally."

Liv is smiling politely, lips frozen in place.

"What can we do for you?" Greg asks.

I have a spiel prepared, using the best dot points on my CV as an alibi. I'm a student and tutor at the [pause for emphasis] University of Melbourne and I'm conducting research on this area of the city, especially the history of this building. I'm looking into—

"You know Nick Cave?" Greg asks. "A movie with him in it was shot around here."

"Whoa," I say. (Later, I realize he means Nic Cage in the movie *Ghost Rider*.)

"City was different fifty years back. You could get a car park!"

"You should talk to Noel," Graeme says. "Noel was here at the opening."

He rifles through the papers in front of him. Greg asks what he's looking for, heaves his six-and-a-half-foot self to his feet, and joins Graeme at the table to sift through documents. Moses doesn't move. I hover an inch above my seat, as if to get up and help — the process looks upsettingly hard, the men's hands paddling through detritus, spines crooked over the desk, glasses slipping down noses — then sit back down.

Graeme plucks something out of a pile and hands me a photocopied booklet: the program from the opening party of the new lodge — this one — in 1954. The centerfold contains the evening's menu. They ate oysters, soup, poultry and ham with vegetables, apple pie and cream, coffee and lemon, sandwiches and sausage rolls. The night's entertainment included sing-alongs and speeches by members.

The woman from before pokes her head in. I can see another man hovering behind her, grinning, craning to get a glimpse into the office. Greg tells her to go and get Noel. He totters in a few minutes later. He is eighty-ish, wearing a gray check tweed suit, a red pocket kerchief, a maroon and blue tie with a gold tie pin shaped like a tiny set of buffalo horns. He beams at us with the kind of non-specific warmth old men reserve for the entire subset of neatly dressed young women.

"When we moved in," Noel begins, "the building had a dirt floor." He leans closer, conspiratorial. I nod, pen poised above notepad. "There were car parks all around, which was very convenient." The other three men nod solemnly.

"I think it was a printing factory before us. Or a stables."

Greg interrupts: "They paid something like fifty grand back then. A pittance."

Noel chuckles. "I'll tell you something."

In the early 1950s, he says, every Victorian member agreed to pay 10 shillings toward the new lodge at Sutherland Street — all but the Richmond branch. They already had their own hall, purchased with their own members' fees and donations. The lodges argued back and forth, and still the Richmond lodge refused to chip in. Eventually, they were ousted from the Buffaloes: barred from participating in any official business or affiliating themselves with RAOB.

Noel, eyes gleaming: "They didn't come to the party. So they were put in the red book."

But the Richmond chapter still wouldn't back down. They continued to operate under the Buffalo name, even recruiting new members, who found themselves unable to attend meetings at other lodges or inter-lodge meetups. When the lodge eventually folded and the members attempted to sell their assets, they saw that the building was legally owned by their treasurer. He had used their money to buy it in his own name.

I ask for more details but Noel is apparently done, sitting back satisfied in his chair.

6.

Whenever I try to steer the conversation back to the building's history, the men start sighing and talking about car parks. I have to find out about the past tenants myself.

The Buffalo Club

The man who bought 22 Sutherland Street in 2018 is Aviv Kheir, better known as "Ozzie" Kheir, a Melbourne-based businessman most famous for owning and part-owning several Melbourne Cup–winning racehorses. His company, Resimax, is one of Australia's largest privately owned property groups. (To give you a sense of scale: in one twenty-four-hour period in December 2015, Resimax purchased $50 million worth of commercial property.) Kheir is also known for his luxury nightclubs and hotels in Melbourne's CBD, one of which, Bond, was the setting of a 2016 reality TV show called *Clubland* that followed socialites and promoters as they attempted to launch the club. In the show, the socialites are women with puffy, collapsing faces, and the promoters all men, whose arms in shirtsleeves look like socks stuffed with tennis balls. In *Clubland*, Kheir wore T-shirts and an eyebrow ring and earrings in both ears, but he seems to favor dark blue suits and V-necks in his professional photos. I call Resimax to see if I can convince someone to persuade Kheir to talk to me, but the receptionist puts me on hold until eventually the line goes dead. Last I heard, he intends to refit 22 Sutherland Street as a dumpling restaurant and karaoke bar.

Before Kheir came Hugo. In 2010, Hugo had been working at a bar in the city—dark and divey, with a forgiving liquor license—and had a feeling there would be others like it. He walked around the city with a paper map, crossing off areas as he visited each one. On the third day, he helped an elderly man across the road. They started chatting, reached the man's destination. Hugo looked up. Above the door, a dirty white sign:

<u>R. A. O. B. G.A.B.</u>
City Temple
25's & Over Club
LIVE Bands 50s & 60s Rock
Friday & Saturday Nights
Y LICENCED Y

He went inside with the man. "Then it just got better and better," he says.

They had a twenty-four-hour liquor license and a space available upstairs. Off the main section, there was a green-tiled hallway, some RAOB regalia high up on the walls, a trophy cabinet. As long as he did the initiation, the committee agreed to rent it to him for a one-off event for "really cheap." How cheap?

"Cheap enough."

The event was a success and he became a full-time tenant. This time, he won't tell me how much rent he paid.

Awkward pause: "Probably shouldn't disclose."

Before Hugo, the upper floor was leased by a karate instructor — "the biggest shark I ever met." When Hugo moved in, the instructor didn't move out.

"This used to be the dojo, man," he liked to say. "I could karate chop you right now and you'd be dead."

Not necessarily an idle threat; the instructor was 6'2", a white guy in track pants and a food-stained singlet. He and Hugo faced off for days, Hugo walking around trying to get rid of him, the instructor making up pretenses for staying. Some years before, the Buffaloes had discussed selling the upper floor to the instructor for a pittance, ballpark figure of $250K. (Hugo suspects he was taking advantage of the most ancient members.) The instructor had turned down the offer at the time, but now told Hugo he was intending to buy. He announced that he would be taking over management of Hugo's future nightclub. Hugo came back with a lawyer in a suit and the instructor finally left.

Before Hugo and the karate instructor, there's rumors Sutherland Street hosted another nightclub, but I haven't been able to find out any details, save that it might have been called "The Mouse Trap." The building's first recorded occupation was in 1866, but, again, there is no information on what it was used for or who owned it. The earliest information I can find is from 1905, when it was the SF Sharp Clothing Factory; in 1925, it was a steel merchants' called Search & Houston; and in the 1940s, it housed the Melbourne General Cleaning Company. The Buffaloes bought the lodge in 1954 for £51,500, and sold it at auction in March 2018 for $6.25 million.

And before all of this, Elizabeth Street — just around the corner from Sutherland — was water, a tributary of Birrarung, the Yarra River. Along its banks and dotted around it were sacred Wurundjeri sites. European invaders built over the tributary to create a stormwater drain and the main road in the 1830s. Along Elizabeth Street today there are tram tracks, motorcycle stores, party shops, $10 haircuts, a juice stand, bars, retail giants, buskers and more, but stand in the right spot and you can still hear the water gurgling beneath you.

7.

Within two months of Hugo's initiation, the upstairs opened as The Buffalo Club. This was in late 2010. He went to meetings for a month or two—he and some other friends who joined to help out with the club—but gradually dropped off. They were always at inopportune times, weekday afternoons, and were "incredibly antiquated" (Hugo makes an inarticulate grizzling sound, old man vocal fry). He says that the nightclub and the Buffaloes maintained a good relationship. He would invite the Buffaloes up early in the night and give them beers: the old men in suits, wasted, mingling with the arriving clubbers.

If there's any truth to the rumor that the Buffaloes is or was a secret gay club, there's a nice symmetry to this. Over the years, Hugs became one of Melbourne's most beloved queer clubs, celebrated for and by its outlandish clientele. Because it was both lawless and right in the middle of the over-policed city center, it felt like a fluke. It was all in the liquor license. "The Buffalo Club" operated as a subsidiary of RAOB, with patrons required to sign up online beforehand or at the door, meaning that thousands of Melbourne's clubbers are also—absurdly—social members of RAOB, meaning that I am a member of RAOB, and that despite its declining real-life membership RAOB Grand Australia Banner is, on paper, one of the largest members-only clubs in the Southern Hemisphere. Police came often, outraged, then more so once they saw the license and realized that, technically, the nightclub was operating entirely within the law. Currently in Melbourne, there is a freeze on applications for liquor licenses seeking to trade after 1 a.m. Hugo recently scoped new locations in the city but licenses like the Buffaloes had are now prohibitively expensive and extremely rare. (Recently, a new club opened up in the CBD and was licensed until 7 a.m. Then, abruptly, it began to shut at 1 a.m.; it turned out the owner had mistaken the 1 for a 7 in the licensing documents.)

A few years back, Hugo thought of buying the building himself, but by then the Buffaloes wanted $5 million for it. They had a long-term vision to sell it for around $6 million.

"Probably should have done it and flipped it a year later for a million more," he says, "but I didn't have that kind of money."

He says this nonchalantly, as though he almost had that kind of money. He is at ease with numbers. He spent around $100K renovating the upstairs area, getting it up to code — it hadn't been upgraded since the 1940s — which involved raising the entire staircase, fixing the roof, and installing fire-safety necessities like smoke alarms, push doors, and emergency lighting. He imagines that the Buffaloes are using their profits to continue trying to exist, putting their money in low-risk investments, maybe 4–5 percent return; that's $250K profit to play with every year.

Hugo still doesn't understand why they let it happen — his voice goes a little dreamy as he speculates. He had "some kind of resemblance of a contract" with the committee, and when newer members joined and took over management, maybe they "understood there was an understanding."

Here's how Greg tells it: "My predecessor" — Greg pulls his mouth down and eyebrows up, signaling irreverence — "drew up a lease on an A4 sheet of paper. By hand."

He lists the numbers one by one. Greg says Hugo paid [redacted] a month, and did not pay for utilities. In the last few months of Hugs, this cost the Buffaloes [redacted].

"You'd go up there and they'd left the freezer open overnight."

Hugo told Greg he was clearing [redacted] a year in profits. Greg says that Hugo said that, with profits like those, he had no intention of leaving; he still had several years left on the contract and intended to use them. If the Buffaloes had stayed in the city, Greg estimates they would have gone bankrupt within three years, paying the council rates and subsidizing Hugs, and all the other costs of running the Buffs. Plus, the Brothers were getting older and had a hard time getting into the city. But they couldn't sell the lodge with Hugo in it. RAOB considered going through the courts to get him out, but that would have been a couple of hundred thousand going to lawyers. In the end, they paid Hugo out to break the lease.

"We lost a lot of money to him," he says simply.

When I go back to Hugo to relay Greg's version of events, he tells me that he and the Buffaloes signed a confidentiality agreement during the end-of-lease negotiations, that the Buffaloes themselves are the ones who wanted the agreement, and that the details about money and the terms of the lease will have to be redacted. When we first spoke, it was just after Hugs had closed and I had perhaps caught him in a particular mood, riding on the afterglow of the final party. This time, he wants to set the record straight.

"We did have a lease," he says. "It was handwritten at first, but then it was *typed up* into a formal document before it was signed."

Hugo says that he and the predecessor in question, the one Greg seems to disdain, got along well. For seven years, everything ran smoothly. But when the new leadership took over, "It was like they had an agenda to sell the building and didn't really care who got hurt in the wash of it."

He doesn't know exactly what happened, but thinks that the old leadership didn't tell the new Buffs about the lease. When they discovered, halfway through the process, having already put the building up for auction, that Hugo did in fact have a formal agreement, they were left red-faced. By then, the club was holding regular events and only just starting to become profitable.

But Hugo didn't want to go through the courts either. He accepted the Buffaloes' offer and moved out a few months later.

"I really felt like it was cut short. I was depressed for so long after, like it was a waste. I play it down to people, but it was a pretty tough road. Dealing with the council, the police, criminal damages, abuse from patrons we kicked out, a leaky roof."

People Who Lunch

You get used to grand old institutions folding, gentrified out of existence by upstart kids. But that's not quite how this story goes. Though the Buffs are leaving the city, they have earned enough from the sale of the building to reproduce themselves ten times over, provided they manage to attract new members. Kheir, the new owner, is now in possession of a rapidly appreciating five-hundred-square-meter warehouse. Even Hugo made some money from the payout. The biggest losers in all of this are the clubbers, the people who went to Hugs religiously every weekend.

"A community of people who felt underrepresented called it home," Hugo says. "That was a source of pride for me. I didn't mean for Hugs to be a queer space from day one, but my intention was that it should be open to whoever invested time and energy into making it great, and that was the community that ended up really caring about it."

"And the freezers?" I ask.

"Firstly, they were refrigerators, and of course we left them open. They were off! You don't leave them closed during the week otherwise they're moldy when you reopen on Thursday."

*

Moses shifts in his chair (he's still staring at us), pats his chest pocket, and leaves the room, presumably to smoke. I can tell the other men want to get back to the party, but I want to keep talking. I still don't know exactly what the Buffaloes *do* — why or how they exist. Every need it meets could be met more fully and more efficiently by other means: cloak-and-daggers ritual by the Freemasons; insurance by insurance agencies; socializing through a church, or an RSL, or a sporting team, or work, or university; workplace protection by a union. Many storied clubs shed their rituals, their costumes, and their lodges in the late twentieth century, transforming into anodyne financial institutions. To give just one example, the company Australian Unity grew out of the fraternity the Independent Order of Oddfellows in the 1840s, and began as a social and business club for members; it now offers health insurance, financial advice, investment portfolios, and aged care living. Still, the Buffaloes persist largely unchanged, preserved as if in an airless pocket.

"What happens at meetings?" I ask Greg.

He seems nonplussed by the question and tells me, as if it's the most obvious thing in the world, "feasting, housekeeping, and fundraising for charities."

They often hold in-house events for specific charities, democratically nominated, with entertainment provided by members. Along with religion and gambling, politics are strictly banned from discussion in the lodges.

"The Brothers might tell some yarns," he says. "Some of them play instruments. We might have a bit of a sing."

The meetings were torturously long, Hugo had said, and I wonder if this is partly the point. Maybe the Buffaloes don't care about efficiency. Probably, inefficiency — or what it allows — is

a pleasure in itself. I'm sure it feels good to while away an afternoon maundering through old songs, the same way it feels good
to spend a night dancing at a club, the next day sleeping, the
next day coming down.

By unspoken agreement, we get to our feet. The men hang
back, letting us go first, Greg holding the door open. We hover in
the foyer, waiting for them to lead; we don't want to go in without a buffer.

8.

In the main hall, nothing happens that I can point to. It's not
like everybody stares, all at once. But there's a rift. White noise;
everyone tunes in. I can see that Liv feels it too by the way her
movements suddenly become very precise and understated.
The hall is a long rectangle filled with skinny wooden laminate
tables around which sit about fifty or so people, most with pots
or cans of beer in front of them. (Greg hands us both tinnies.)
Down the middle of the tables, there are plastic bowls filled
with snacks. The room, which is toward the back of the building and so shares walls with other buildings, is either windowless or almost entirely windowless; if there were windows, let
the record show that it felt windowless. There's no music playing, just loud conversation and raucous laughter bouncing
between six wooden surfaces.

I can see two women here. The paper-bag drinker from
before, and a woman drinking a Coke and wearing a floral shirt.
Heni is the paper-bag drinker. She is pouring clear liquid into a

tumbler and drinking it straight. She pulls the bag down to show me the vodka label, and winks. Every time I talk to her, she dissolves into wheezing laughter. She is from New Zealand, Māori, and might be the only non-white person here. Michelle is on call for her job as a coach driver and is not drinking. She recently injured her knee picking up toys from the bus floor and is waiting for WorkCover to come through. I ask what they think of the all-male thing. Heni wheeze-laughs.

"It's great," Michelle says.

Heni, cackling: "Stops them bothering us for two seconds."

"They're all getting older now. Gives them something to look forward to."

I go to find the bathroom and emerge in the other foyer, the entrance to Hugs off the unnamed lane. Someone has parked their mobility scooter at the foot of the stairs, which lead up to the nightclub. Last time I was here, almost exactly a month ago, it was for the final hours of Hugs' closing party. I went alone, first thing in the morning; it had been going all night. I remember walking upstairs and into the club where a single air-conditioner huffed at the spilled drinks, cigarette smoke, wet tiles, amyl fumes, and hundreds of sweating bodies. It was January, and I had expected heat, but this was something else; I walked toward the dance floor, crossed some invisible threshold, and was soaked. By 11 a.m., the final few minutes, the DJ booth was packed with half-stripped people wearing expressions of pained euphoria, the dance floor the same. Half an hour later, we all stood in the alleyway blinking and smoking and dripping before scattering into the summer morning.

I'm back from the bathroom just in time for the speeches. Noel retells the story of the Richmond lodge grifter to the assembled crowd, word for word, while I sit on the side of the stage and write down all the shoes I can see. New Balances, incongruous skate shoes, leather boaters, suede boaters, polished black dress shoes (Noel), a *lot* of New Balances, actually, as well as unbranded puffy white sneakers. Only a few suits today, mostly on the truly ancient. One man is wearing a sky-blue button-down shirt, made of thick satin fabric rolling with light. There are several of the black polos embroidered with "RAOB," jean shorts, droopy gray cardigans made of coarse wool, thin cotton dress shirts. There is, right in front of me, a tremendously long gray rat-tail, unfurling from a balding head, hanging down over the chair's back, its length partitioned by colorful elastic bands.

I feel the column of my spine pull up when Graeme, in his speech, mentions "two very special guests," but of course he doesn't mean us, he means some interstate Buffaloes. Applause, laughter. The room begins to break apart. People are brought to us like gifts. Noel points out his brother Bill, full name William James Dunstan, who is ninety-four years old and drinking a glass of beer. He is the same age as the other oldest member, Jeff Hugo, also here, in a gray suit with only a couple of stains on it.

Jeff Hugo leans over to Liv and says, "We've got to stop meeting like this."

Several men haul him to his feet and hold him up next to Bill for a photo that they have insisted Liv would like to take. In the photograph, Jeff is bisected by two hairy arms clasped around his chest.

Jeff asks Liv: "What are you doing Wednesday night? I'll pick you up at 8?"

Everyone is getting drunker, us included, and it's only 4 p.m. Liv is surrounded by several men; I'm talking to the man with the rat's tail. I feel frustrated that I won't find out anything this way, my own presence obstructing the view. Is this a mystery anyone wants solved? Is it even a mystery? Everyone is telling the same story: brotherhood, brought in by an uncle or a mate, sad to see the lodge go, been a member for twenty-five years. There might be nothing more to it than what we see.

I sit down at one of the tables, alone except for a man at the opposite end, staring into the middle distance. We ignore each other companionably. The tabletops are scattered with half-finished plates of food, and for the first time I notice what they've been eating: jelly snakes, Kingstons, Monte Carlos, Scotch Fingers, yellow crinkle-cut chips, ham sandwiches made on white bread and cut into small strips, jelly beans, mini sausage rolls. I feel a wave of despair, related to the food but not *of* the food, and I don't know whether it's because all this will pass (the subject of another reality series, perhaps, Ozzie Kheir gutting the building but keeping the buffalo painting for character) or because it hasn't yet passed, should have passed years ago.

The Beautiful Piece

There is a magazine from Melbourne that publishes book reviews online. It promises that these are innovative and unlike other book reviews. A brief survey reveals a formula: personal experience is fused to an analysis of the book, often in a paragraph-by-paragraph oscillation. Sometimes, instead of the personal, the reviewer tag-teams their analysis with theory: queer, literary, critical race, affect, feminist. More ambitious works will throw in a third term. For instance, a recent piece has three components —

A [theory]

B [analysis of book]

C [personal experience]

— in which the writer's experience of trauma inflects their reading of the text on trauma and both are informed by a theory of representing pain. Here is what the review looks like when mapped paragraph by paragraph:

A, A, B, C, B, B, B, B, A/B, A, A, B, B, A/B/C

Here is the second most recent review: C, C B, B, C, C, B, C, B, B, B, C, C, C/B

And another: C, C, B, C, C, B, B, C, C

And finally: CX8, BX12

In the first two reviews, the Cs also contain As and Bs, some Bs contain As, and so on — content leaks across form. In the final two, each line of inquiry is sealed hermetically in paragraphs or sections and the reader is left to infer or produce their relationships. Two forms — one allusory, a tight interweaving of sources and concepts, often lyrically disposed; the other, fragmentary, disjointed — and two ways of synthesizing texts. In the former, the writer has already done most of this work, while in the latter, the task of synthesis falls more heavily to the reader. An example of the former might be Maggie Nelson's *The Argonauts*, and the latter, also by Nelson, *Bluets*.

At readings — in dark-paneled pubs, bowls clubs, gentrified bars, white-cube galleries, beer-humid function rooms — these forms are on high rotation: long personal essay intellectualizing Carly Rae Jepson, lyric essay on museums and the fragment, childbirth memoir plus Cixous. The formula holds in little and big magazines, bestsellers, and art-imprint obscurities alike: goshawk plus grief, a text on mania unfolding in fragments knitting together film and literary criticism, "a seamless blend of memoir, cultural history, literary criticism, and journalistic reportage" (blurb for Leslie Jamison's *The Recovering*, 2018), "her own brand of essay-meets-prose poetry about identity and culture" (for Durga Chew-Bose's *Too Much and Not the Mood*, 2017), a trip through "illuminating material from literature, art, philosophy, psychology, pop culture, and more" (for Marina Benjamin's *Insomnia*, 2018), a text that moves from "critical theory to pop culture to the intimacies and plain exchanges of daily life" (for Maggie Nelson's *On Freedom*, 2021). I read the latest para-academic-queer-autotheory blockbuster and all I got was this eccentric combination of texts applied to the quotidian.

In his hybrid essay for *Texte Zur Kunst* (September 2016 issue), poet and critic Felix Bernstein parodies the eccentricity of the hybrid essay, for instance, the kind that might be published by *Texte Zur Kunst*:

> As I wrote this I was listening to *x* on iTunes, friend *x* called, we read *x* quote from theory, I had sad memory *x* while at *x* gallery, where I came to conclusion *x* about *x* sensibility. Then I proposed and defined an *x+1* sensibility, using timid caution, as apology and alibi to put forward cluster of *x+1* artists, including me.

Bernstein's formula is a millennial redux of what boomer luminaries have been doing for years, exemplary of which is Mary Cappello's advice to creative nonfiction writers (offered in 2016, though her first book of nonfiction was released in 1999):

> Gather together an uncommon archive made of home movies and Wittgenstein, your aunt's rosary beads and father's garden logs, the nubbly surface of memory's grain, the Pocketbooks

that shaped your early adolescence alongside a forgotten literary theorist of your choice. Incorporate a musical soundtrack
as interlocutionary base and space, then write from there.

There are degrees of self-awareness here; where Cappello is
complacent among the artifacts of a middle-class habitus, Bernstein flounders, aware that he traffics in precisely the currency
he critiques. Nevertheless, Cappello unwittingly illustrates the
tenets of what Bernstein names "the irreproachable essay." His
argument centers around the imperviousness of hybrid texts to
critique. If it's both a memoir and a review, it's neither narcissistic nor making claims to objectivity; if it uses theory to eluci-
date pop culture, it's neither elitist nor shallow — or less likely to
be called so, anyway. Hybridity allows the writer to correct the
perceived deficiencies of one discipline or form with another
discipline or form. This tessellation of form functions alongside
content — "deferential footnotes, astute self-criticism, personal
sentiment, poetic language, and academic theory" (Bernstein) —
to preempt criticism of its elitism, or its complicity with the
institution, or its success in the literary market in order to "create an integrity that is beyond reproach." Bernstein asks: "In
being this irreproachable, have we not fallen into the same old
trap of disciplinary authority?"

Of course, Bernstein does reproach the irreproachable essay,
meaning that it's not exactly irreproachable, not to mention that
by critiquing its imperviousness to critique he a) positions himself above the irreproachable essay, that is, above being irreproachable, which b) positions him as flawed and implicated,
the same maneuver he lampoons in essays that vie for imperviousness therefore vying for imperviousness himself, and c) that

being the first to name and denounce it is a shortcut to disciplinary authority.

But others have convincingly echoed his sentiment. In her review of Leslie Jamison's *The Recovering*, writer Ellena Savage finds that the text preemptively shapes itself in response to anticipated criticism: "What can I say about *The Recovering* that Jamison hasn't already predicted I might say?...its self-knowledge...not only anticipates a diagnosis, but outperforms the diagnostic expert." In a critique that feels almost rudely targeted at Cappello et al. but was written before her and Bernstein's precepts, poetry critic Brian M. Reed argues that "hybrid writing tends to be so skillful, so erudite, that it reads like the prized outcome of the very educational system whose disciplinary logic [the writer] seeks to undermine." The companion to paranoid reading—Eve Kosofky Sedgwick's term for the deconstruction-adjacent practice of reading to expose a text's latent bias—is paranoid writing: writing to get ahead of the paranoid reader, a guns-at-dawn quick-draw to reveal the text's flaws.

In the ultimate recursion, criticism also preempts criticism of its criticism. You never know who will be reading it, who might take exception to your reading, especially if it circulates online. Ever name-searched yourself on Twitter? Ever screenshotted a questionable Insta-story and sent it to a friend? Online, we embed context within the work, loading it with disclaimers and acknowledgments before we post. The hyper-qualified block-text Insta-story is merely the most distilled version of the irreproachable essay. And the irreproachable essay is merely the most distilled version of the essay itself; *essai* means "trial" or "attempt" in the original French—the genre is shaped by its preemptive dissimulation of authority.

*

A tiring form — to read, to write, to critique. This has a lot to do with (my own) overexposure to hybrid writing but more to do with something immanent to the form itself. Hybrid writing is akin to what theorist Sianne Ngai identifies as the strenuous play of zaniness: a form of amusement edged with frenzy. Zaniness indexes failure insofar as the performer's varied attempts to perform displays only their attempts, thereby falling short of a performance. Zaniness is a failure that doesn't rise to the status of a "queer art" because it remains wedded to success, no ironic distance available. Many of Jim Carrey's characters — the cable guy and the workaholic father from *Liar Liar* — are "zanies," and their elasticity in response to precarity and hyperemployment is exemplary of the just-barely-keeping-it-together aesthetic of zaniness. Lucille Ball of *I Love Lucy* is a zany, thirsting for show business and undertaking a series of complicated plots to get there. The freelance writer is a zany, often casually employed to support their practice, attempting to sell stories, essays, and books, stranded somewhere between the better-moneyed academic and art worlds, locked out of insurance and leave and represented, if at all, by a patchwork of unions ill-adapted for contemporary arts work — there's no one project or job, no one source of income, no mandated routine, no regular workplace. Zaniness is precisely this: an aesthetic of overwork as play. (I run into a friend's ex from a non-relationship in the library of a uni neither of us attends, a guy I thought of as zany long before I read Ngai, mid-morning on a Thursday, and he tells me about his project: he gathers multiple texts, opens each of them at random and reads transversally, skipping from book to book, to see what connections emerge.)

Ngai is obviously describing the post-Fordist worker, one who produces social relationships and affects, and the incorporation of affect, personality, and play into existing work structures. Part of this paradigm is what we could call predictive labor: the labor of preempting needs, requests, possible problems; of making oneself available and responsive. (Preempting the labor to come is work in itself.) As well as actually doing the odd jobs and tasks, managing them — continually re/arranging conflicting commitments into temporary stability — is an invisible part of contemporary work, and concealing this work is also part of the job. Case in point: the scheduling bot "Amy Ingram," who impressed users with her humanlike tone and skill set, turned out to have a team of human workers behind her, covering for oversights and inflecting her communications with human warmth. But where the Mechanical (Digital?) Turk hides its sweating human substrate, zaniness places it front and center. Arguably, making the invisible visible is a defining feature of zaniness, whose drama and comedy come precisely from exaggerating the laboriousness of synthesizing, or from bungling the attempt at concealment so badly that you only increase its visibility.

When I read a hybrid text, perhaps I react sourly to Ngai's version of zaniness: not a work's obvious quirks, its slide across disciplines and forms, but hybridity's shadowing by the ludicrous position of the hybrid writer (of me) — and most writers, unless wealthy or funded, are hybrid entities by necessity. If hybridity is a new form of mastery, as Bernstein suggests, seeming to cede authority while actually consolidating it, it is also precarity in action; its mastery is visibly unstable, temporary, unsettled, its attentions in-demand and split. The freelance writer is a supplicant with a pitch, competing with a thousand others just like them, diversifying their wheelhouse to meet any possible brief. At its most alienated, the hybrid text is an outcome of conflicting demands, using a combinatorial logic to create novelty and scarcity in an attention economy — a modular specificity that can be undone and reconstituted as needed in an attempt to corner a market. The hybrid text indexes a hopeless in-between that is not outside the status quo, a challenge to the institution or labor market, but of it. Ngai again: hybridity as the "weakening of art's capacity to serve as an image of non-alienated labor."

*

This isn't quite the full picture. Anne Carson, we know, divides her writing time between three different desks in three different rooms for three different projects. Writing for pay is hardly the worst job going, and though fraught with exploitation, writing for literary magazines or within an institution is generally far better work than writing content or clickbait, let alone, say, dying a personal heat-death in an unventilated Amazon warehouse or collecting rubbish at a Work for the Dole site in rural Queensland. Even as the text reveals its precarious conditions of production, even as the writer dissimulates their authority and prestige, the form — how can it not? — carries and imparts a certain status. As Cappello and Bernstein's formulas make clear, hybrid texts are sometimes little more than celebrations of the writer and their good, educated, erudite tastes (after all, knowing when to concede and when to dissimulate this prestige is perhaps the ultimate marker of good taste).

If you take Michel de Montaigne as the originator of the form, or at least the name for the form, the essay's patrician tendencies will come as no surprise. In 1571, the story goes, Montaigne retired from public life to a tower in his family's castle in Bordeaux (like all good freelancers, Montaigne worked from home). He had been a counselor in Parliament and a courtier for Charles XI. His family were landed gentry, with a large estate and income from the salt-herring and wine trades. It's thought that the loss of his closest friend, the writer and judge Étienne de La Boétie, inspired Montaigne to write as a "means of communication" where "the reader takes the place of the dead friend." He wrote in the first person, on all subjects, from idleness to cannibalism, but his real topic was himself: "I myself am the matter of my book." By exploring the depths of the self, he characterized the self as something that had depth and could be explored, dramatizing the process of self-fashioning, which was inextricable from essaying. He wrote that to *essai* is "to follow a movement so wandering as that of our mind, to penetrate the opaque depths of its innermost folds, to pick out and immobilize the innumerable flutterings that agitate it."

Here you can see several key ingredients of the essay as it will develop, not least among them its long association with wealth and status: the essay as a conversational, convivial, intimate medium, alive and fleet-footed; the essay as almost definitionally personal; less generously, narcissistic; the essay as something "occasioned" by a particular situation; the essay as a genteel pastime for learned gentlemen, especially in their twilight years (the weirdly tenacious connection between retirement and the essay deserves an essay of its own); and the essay as a form that habitually reflects on its own construction as a form within itself.

Any essay origin-story that starts with Montaigne can't avoid stumbling, almost immediately, into the obvious and somewhat inconvenient fact that essays have always been hybrid, therefore rendering the term "hybrid essay" a tautology. I could prove this with recourse to several examples drawn from one of the many door-stopper anthologies of the essay, say, *The Oxford Book of Essays* (1625–1980), and explicate, for instance, Henry David Thoreau's "Night and Moonlight" (1862), but suffice to say that if A = reflection and analysis, B = references and discussion of references (to literature, philosophy, and science), and C = personal experience, the first three pages of "Night and Moonlight" look like this, beginning, as many essays do, in the personal:

C, B, A, A, A, A, B/A, A, A/B, A/B, A, C

There is a problem of causality here, both for genre-bending zealots and for my argument. If the essay has always been hybrid, is it possible to claim that the contemporary hybrid essay has anything to do with precarity? (Likewise, zaniness comes from around the fourteenth century in Italy — from the commedia dell'arte, a form of theater, which included the stock character of a cunning trickster known as a *Zanni*.) We frequently imagine that genre works by reiterating, with variation, an original form. But the essay has not been piped directly from Montaigne to Thoreau to the creative writing workshop. The essay of a rural English rector in 1680 is different from the essay of a cosmopolitan English philosopher in 1680 is different from the essay of an English journalist in 1680, and so on, ad infinitum. There is no monolithic Essay that all essays conform to or rebel against (and you would expect nothing less of a form characterized by its variety). This is partly what makes the discourse around genre-bending so maddening; positioning a text as genre-transgressive often reinstates the primacy of genre, or inflates its supposed grip on older texts and epochs in order to stage the transgression.

So the answer cannot be found by looking at the essay on its own, the essay written by an individual and read by an individual, or even a whole range of essays; it can only be found by examining the form's production and circulation within a given milieu. The earliest essays were collected and printed in books; the advent of the newspaper and periodical in the seventeenth century disarticulated the book and encouraged the production of stand-alone essays; the Internet accelerates this disarticulation, disseminating texts further and faster than ever before. Though the essay has always been hybrid, the essay's hybridity is now being put to new uses. Far from its rarefied origins and its rarefied present — its long five minutes of fame in the anglophone literary world — the hybrid text is now so familiar, so ubiquitous, that we barely even notice we're reading it.

*

I'm talking about clickbait — a kind of canary-in-the-coal-mine for literary alienation, the most reviled of online content, the biggest online grift since a million Nigerian princes sent a million requests for alms. If you've spent any time online, you will know it intimately. Clickbait is content that exists primarily to garner clicks, likes, subscriptions, and, ultimately, advertising revenue. It is content that promises big with its headline — "3 Simple Steps to Shed Belly Fat After 40"; "This Man Tried to Hug A Wild Lion. You Won't Believe What Happened Next" — and fails to deliver in content: we lose fat by cutting out sugar; the man does not get devoured by the lion. I'm going to include in this category clickbait-adjacent media, content that uses similar or identical tactics for a similar or identical goal, even if concealed by a more dignified frame; no matter how they distinguish themselves (*Junkee*, the Australian pop culture and news site, calls its material "clickable" rather than clickbait), the difference is one of degree rather than kind.

Consider, then, clickbait and content as hybrid forms. For instance, each *Junkee* or *BuzzFeed* article is *Junkee/BuzzFeed* in miniature: a combination of images, reportage, memes, opinion, video, articles, native advertising (ads formatted and worded to mimic the non-paid content exactly), and a first-person narrative voice. As on the parent page, which presents content in a grid formation that unfurls as you scroll, the unique page doesn't have an endpoint; the article finishes and a new one takes its place, so that the borders between content are blurry, basically nonexistent.

This aesthetic is coterminous with the structural zaniness of the content writer's position. Picture Anne Carson squared to the power of one hundred desks, Montaigne but terminally online. *Junkee* staff work in staggered shifts, publishing a certain number of articles in their allotted time to produce a twenty-four-hour feed. Writers for "churnalism" sites — sites that churn out news and gossip, often recycled from other outlets — must work at a rapid clip to make a living: anything from two to ten articles a day is standard. Content mills, sometimes known as content factories or content farms (choose your own nostalgic euphemism), employ a huge network of writers, sometimes paid and on staff, sometimes unpaid interns, more frequently freelancers paid a tremendously low rate per article, to produce content based on key search terms. These articles exist only to drive traffic to the site and increase its ranking on Google; sometimes, they are not even meant to be read and are hidden in out-of-the way links on the page, or published as transparent keyword-stuffed text that is picked up by search terms but invisible to readers. On the other side of production, click farms use a combination of bots and low-paid workers to endlessly generate fake accounts that like, subscribe, and retweet to make content go viral, boost the lackluster metrics of a politician or wannabe influencer, or, in the case of scams, lend it a veneer of legitimacy. It's thought that over 60 percent of all online traffic in 2021 was driven by bots.

Under these conditions, content writers can't afford to cultivate and indulge niche interests over several months, or even several hours. The industry demands of its workers not just the ability to write about anything speedily and efficiently, but the ability to speedily and efficiently switch from writing about one thing to writing about the next. Working across subjects and themes, writers deploy the house tone to maintain the coherence of the publication and brand. Or perhaps more accurately, given that clickbait's overt zaniness is the source of its identity and identifiability, the incoherence maintains the publication's coherency. *Junkee* staff's bylines straddle the site's categories of TV, film, music, politics, and culture; a writer pitches two articles in the morning, posts on the deportation of a refugee family before lunch, and writes about the trailer for *Cats* in the afternoon. In its early days, *BuzzFeed* was governed entirely by an algorithm aggregating content that showed signs of going viral. Founder Jonah Peretti eventually hired "curators" (his word) to spotlight and structure the most popular content into listicles. Writers and editors came last. *BuzzFeed*'s aesthetic — overwhelming, hyperactive, busy — exists in and because of its aggregative nature, its zaniness produced by the algorithm's synthesizing function, its synthesizing function reproduced by its writers.

So, despite an appearance of whimsy, the freelancer tossing off takes as they marinate online, content is produced within strict parameters. Search any content style guide or SEO advice blog — search Google with confidence, knowing that the top results will have been optimized, that the page therefore knows its stuff (SEO gets high off its own fumes) — and you will find detailed instructions on how to reproduce the form.

The same goes for clickbait, especially its most infamous constituent part, its metonymic emissary, the headline. I know of at least four headline-generator tools, two headline-evaluators, including one that scores for emotional impact, countless AI clickbait-writers in varying states of sophistication and, of course, the language model known as GPT (which is a whole other story). And while there is no universal formula for its production, these tools work off general principles; if there *were* a universal formula, it would have to do with its tenaciousness as a form despite the lack of a universal formula.

Consider the following headlines:

"The 7 Craziest Things Bella Thorne Wore at Coachella"

"Marvel's Golden Boy and Excellent Person Taika Waititi Might Be Taking a Role in 'Suicide Squad'"

"The New Lana Del Rey Album Is Here, and It's Everything You Want From a Lana Del Rey Album"

These aren't the most egregious examples—there are no weight-loss hacks, no man-eating lions—but they are recognizably clickbait, even when pulled from their contexts and transplanted here. You will immediately notice a few commonalities: that the sentence is in title case (the first letter of every major word capitalized); that they are packed with names and numbers; that they rely on Internet parlance and pop-culture references; and that the sentences tend to be lengthy.

These are important features of clickbait. But dig a little deeper and you will find that what makes clickbait clickbait is syntax—its particular way of building sentences. First, where traditional headlines offer paratactic collages ("Police Car Rammed Altona"; "Hottest Day Since April, Bureau Reports"), clickbait headlines are usually full sentences, grammatically complete.

Second, they contain a high proportion of what are known, coincidentally, as content words. Unlike function words—words that stitch a sentence together—content words point to concrete objects or phenomena, offering information and meaning. Adjectives, verbs, adverbs, and nouns are content words; prepositions ("in," "at"), conjunctions ("and," "but"), auxiliary verbs ("do," "has"), articles ("the," "a"), and pronouns ("she," "he") are function words. In the news headlines above, there are no function words; in the clickbait headlines, the function words remain—the sentences are complete—but they are far outnumbered by content words. For instance, the Waititi headline contains five nouns, two adjectives or adjective phrases, and three forms of verbs, leaving only two function words ("and" and "a"):

> "Marvel's Golden Boy [possessive noun, adjective, noun] and [conjunction] Excellent Person Taika Waititi [adjective phrase, proper noun] Might Be Taking a Role in 'Suicide Squad' [modal verb phrase, verb, noun, proper noun]"

Third, clickbait tends to have long "syntactic dependencies"—the space that closes a dependent clause, for instance, the number of words between the first mention of the subject of the sentence and the verb that conveys the subject's action. The dependency is the held breath, the anticipation you feel as you read toward a full stop. In this example, the dependency is created by the drawn-out description of the Waititi:

> "[Marvel's Golden Boy and Excellent Person Taika Waititi = subject] Might Be [Taking = verb] a Role in 'Suicide Squad'"

Finally, they often use cataphora, a word or phrase that refers to a later word or phrase:

> "[Marvel's Golden Boy and Excellent Person = cataphor] [Taika Waititi = referent] Might Be Taking a Role in 'Suicide Squad'"

Clickbait wants its readers to do one thing—click the link—and every element of the headline is honed to produce this result. If clickbait was a film, it would be a B-grade thriller; its syntax is structured for suspense. Cataphora, dependencies, and content words create plots or premises in miniature, giving the reader a protagonist with character traits and a mystery to solve: an abbreviated arc that sends the reader down the sentence and into the link. It withholds action from both its subject (Waititi) and reader until the last moment, then unleashes it all at once ("Might Be Taking a Role") or — in more obvious examples — promises its revelation on the next page ("You Won't Believe What Happens Next").

To show just how important these are in clickbait, let's take them away. By paring back these sentences to their barest structures, we will see how a form can approximate formlessness — and by extension, see what clickbait shares with the essay.

Here's the Waititi headline rewritten as a newspaper headline: as an incomplete sentence, with minimal content words, short dependencies, and without cataphora:

"Taika Waititi Takes Role in 'Suicide Squad' "

Flat, factual, and stripped of adjectives, it now reads like a Hemingway six-worder, a nigh-unrecognizable abstraction from its overwrought, Foster-Wallacian source material. On the other hand, if you remove the headline's nouns, proper nouns, and numbers, swapping them out for a placeholder —

"Marvel's Golden Boy and Excellent Person Taika Waititi Might Be Taking a Role in 'Suicide Squad' "=

"[0] Might Be Taking a [0] in [0]"

— its title case —

"[0] might be taking a [0] in [0]"

— and every last one of its content words —

"[0] [0] [0] and [0] [0] [0] [0] a [0] [0]" =

"[PN] [Adj] [N] and [Adj phr] [PN] [MVP] [V] a [N] [PN]"

— you are left with a blueprint whose alien notation belies its familiarity, but which can be used to construct any number of headlines:

"[0] [0] [0] and [0] [0] [0] [0] a [0] [0]" =

"[PN] [Adj] [N] and [Adj phr] [PN] [MVP] [V] a [N] [PN]" =

"[possessive noun, adjective, noun] [conjunction] [adjective phrase, proper noun] [modal verb phrase/infinitive] [verb, possessive determiner, noun, proper noun]" =

"America's Most-Hated President and War Criminal George W. [W.] Bush Might Be Touring His Art Show 'Portraits of Courage'" =

"Maryborough's Famous Children's Author and Mary Poppins Creator P. L. Travers Will Be Getting Her Own Movie 'Saving Mr. Banks'" = (with minor adjustments)

"Area Man's Beloved Wife and Business Partner [proper noun] Has Been Trolling His Business's Facebook Page [proper noun]"

In other words, what matters in clickbait is not the particularities of the content, but the generic nature of the form; stripped of all its old parts with new ones subbed in, it nevertheless retains its identity as clickbait.

This formula allows for the endless generation of new clickbait. It is also what allows clickbait to be detected and blocked. For example, the team behind Stop Clickbait, a browser extension that does what it says in the name, found that it could more accurately filter clickbait from non-clickbait when it based its decisions on sentence patterns rather than key words or common topics—more accurately, even, than a two-pronged approach that took both into account. Once identified, the extension produces a summary of the content, closing the "curiosity gap," the drawn-out non-revelation. Invariably, if you do click the link, the article will be split across several pages, each clogged with advertising, and the final page will deflate the surprise promised by the title, ejecting you back into the ether from which you came: there is no answer, only a continued deferral.

Here, the usual hierarchy is reversed: content is more a vehicle for form than form is for content; each particularity is merely an occasion for replicating the generic. Think of memes and meme formats, of endless iterations of the same joke on Twitter. As long as the form holds, however loosely, the meme, joke, or content will continue to function. In fact, it only becomes funnier the more it changes with repetition, the more abstracted it becomes from its beginnings, the more niche its references, the more disjunctive its syntheses. If, as Ngai writes, "The project augurs its own end" — it is temporary and self-contained, just one of a series of projects that will compose a life's work — content augurs its own endlessness. It is only useful in vast amounts, both for those who make a living writing it (or exploiting those who write it) and for websites that use it to pull in clicks and views. When you click a link that contains another link and you click that link and another one and another one, the boundaries between content — see how the word sounds strange in the singular here, would sound even stranger if you forced the plural "s" as in "contents" — tend to blur. Even when the word "content" is used to describe a single example of content, it alludes to all other content, without which it would not function as content: it would just be — what? An ad? A text? A literary text? An artwork?

If it's difficult to even conceive of content in itself, it's because content is ultimately content-less. A placeholder or a void, it doesn't matter *what* the particular value is, just that there is a particular value. Content is a hybrid form, not just because it combines image, text, art, video, and advertising, but because content is, by nature, capacious to the point of emptiness. Like data, everything online and off can be content; it transforms everything it touches into more of itself. It makes an object into a value that can be exchanged with all other values; it is "the equation of the incompatible," to quote Marx quoting Shakespeare.

You can see what I'm getting at: if content is an empty value, it functions much like a commodity. *Like* a commodity? Online, words *are* commodities. Content is produced on an industrial scale under conditions optimized for exploitation; each word, headline, or article has a measurable numeric value; and each produces surplus value for a corporation or a boss that its makers, for the most part, will never see. More than this, commodification converts the particular into the generic form of value so that it can be exchanged with other chunks of value. To do so, it has to preserve or create the appearance of specificity — I need *this* not *that*, would prefer *that* not *this*.

*

Most writers will strenuously deny that their practice has anything to do with the debased business of content production. In content, writing is overdetermined by its conditions of production; it actively seeks to close the gap between writing and value production by writing to these conditions. Meanwhile, literary writing is often viewed as a kind of unproductive labor — a pleasurable waste of time, a conscientious objection to the furor of overproduction, a non-alienated way of making art. Literariness is determined precisely by its resistance to the instrumentalization of language — of everything — that content represents.

Here's a representative of the above position — Geordie Williamson, in his introduction to *The Best Australian Essays 2015* — anxiously polarizing the forms:

> Wonky, idiosyncratic, fragmentary, paradoxical, drunk on words, the essay has something that the AI algorithms and content-wallahs and social media provocateurs of the web do not: character, style, oomph! — a uniquely human thumbprint that only other thinking people recognize and pen their carefully keylocked attentions for.

This passage is noteworthy for the way it distills many of the essay's foundational conceits. Note, firstly, the obvious: that Williamson's exhortation musters content and the essay into separate enclosures, fortified between. Note that it is an example of the form itself, performing the traits it spruiks: the "oomph" in his rapid-fire stream of adjectives, its wonkiness mimicked by an unevenly tripartite sentence structure, its drunkenness by the volubility of the sentence and the enthusiasm with which it makes it claims, its character in all of the above plus quirks like the exclamation mark. Note that this combination of precision and variation is crucial to the hybrid form, that it displays the effortful effortlessness characteristic of both the hybrid text and the zany subject, and that it also exemplifies the freewheeling, near-maniacal cheer the form's practitioners often display when spruiking the form — as if to detract from the calculated and frequently un-cheery work of producing the illusion in the first place. Finally, note that it opposes the cold "AI algorithms, content-wallahs and social media provocateurs" with the warmth of a uniquely — universally? — "human thumbprint."

What is Williamson so afraid of? Given that most online content, literary or otherwise, is found through a search engine — Google tops the list of most-visited websites in Australia and America year in, year out — it takes some serious blue-pilling to argue that writing remains aloof from its conditions of production, circulation, and consumption; from its competitors on a' crowded playing field (if everyone's doing it, it becomes unsustainable not to do it). *Electric Lit*, for example, has wholeheartedly embraced a clickbait/content model of promotion, aggregating commissioned stories, reading lists, and listicles couched in the language of social justice: "9 Stories About Family Violence," "8 Books to Help You Understand the Kashmir Conflict." *Literary Hub* is a platform that aggregates "the best of the literary internet," acquiring and republishing work from its partners, which include the *Paris Review, n+1*, and Penguin Random House. *The Betoota Advocate*, a satirical Australian news site, has taken native advertising a step further by selling unmarked ad space in the form of articles, its clients buying their own profitable ridicule (and the paper's four-million-strong reach).

Nor have the upper echelons of the literary establishment been spared. A manual parse shows that headlines for *The New Yorker*'s online site don't share clickbait's formula, exactly, but are just as formulaic. It recently favored a "[Determiner] [noun] [preposition] [noun/proper noun]" structure — or translated into the same terms as before, "The [0] of [0]": "The World of Jia Tolentino," "The Survival of Iggy Pop," "The Power of Investigative Journalism," "The Urgency of the 2020 Senate Race," "The Niche Celebrity Satire of 'BH90210,'" "The Message of Measles"; these all appeared within a seven-day window of each other, and I'm not even counting headlines with slight variations. You can try a similar experiment with similar results on *Jacobin*, which appears to be using a soft milling approach, floating its most clickable titles on Twitter — "The Great Socialist Bake Off" — to pull in readers to its altogether more earnest platform.

Headlines and sentences are one thing; whole essays are another. I would like, here, to feed an AI several thousand essay collections, literary memoirs, magazines, stand-alone essays for literary magazines, and anthologies, *The Best Australian Essays 2015* among them. Picture *Printing out the Internet* in reverse, innumerable pages rolling back into the machine. (A friend tells me he could maybe do it if I send him a few thousand documents, but sourcing and tagging the material is a whole project in itself, and anyway, I'm not sure I want to automate this essay out of its job.)

DIY in lieu: a representative anthology of creative nonfiction about creative nonfiction by some of the field's most celebrated writers, *Bending Genre*, edited by Nicole Walker and Margot Singer, and published in 2016. Even without the benefit of a thousands-strong dataset, read a few essays in *Bending Genre* and a rhythm begins to emerge—not necessarily the staccato ABCs of the book reviews, though they are there if you want to track them (Eula Biss's contribution oscillates paragraph by paragraph between meditations on organic farming and lyric essays), but a kind of listing to one side of the topic, a zigzag that starts on the zag. To use a maxim of creative nonfiction, adopted from an Emily Dickinson poem (and popularized by Brenda Miller and Suzanne Paolo's book that takes the phrase as its title), the essayists "tell it slant," often beginning in a tangentially related concept or setting—as usual, personal anecdotes feature heavily here—before shifting focus. There is no single formula that holds across the anthology. Still, as in clickbait, throughout the collection there is a sense of uniformity all the more unsettling because of the essays' apparent diversity. What the texts have in common is their randomness, or potential for it. Fluidity becomes the norm; the uniformity of the essays derives from their insistent specificity, not in spite of it.

Not coincidentally, the writers in the anthology often define their craft in terms of movement. Karen Brennan identifies "a specific *physical* restlessness that motivates the genre-bender" (emphasis hers). In an essay that unfolds in small paragraphs, demarcated by indentations but no line breaks, Wayne Koestenbaum writes that: "Each book, poem, or paragraph I produce is a physical machine, generated by hand movements. I like to put my fingers to work." Dinty W. Moore writes on "the energy of the jump" conducted by line breaks, spaces, and other interruptions to the text, and uses these liberally throughout. Not in *Bending Genre* but in a collection of essays called *Nilling*, Lisa Robertson writes that "[e]njambment is the counter-semiotic pause within the rhythmic gesture. It knows that the temporal unit is sprung on the refusal of the regularization of time, which must remain situated in the body, as the body's specificity, its revolt."

Here, hybrid nonfiction preemptively subverts what it imagines are the expected rhythms of nonfiction prose. Like Williamson, it looks to the implicitly human body to guide this subversion, to offer a counter-rhythm. But is this the rhythm of the body (whose body, where?) or is it the rhythm of the body, say, on Twitter, the shot attention span briefly clamping on fragments of information as it glides down the feed? Is this a "counter-semiotic pause," or is it a staff writer at *BuzzFeed* grabbing a dinner break at midnight? Are the working fingers hovering over a typewriter in a light-filled studio, or are they in a click-farm in Hangzhou, hitting a laptop's trackpad in repetitive spasms? Have you noticed, lately, that the most ruthlessly optimized content is written in an arrhythmic mix of one-, two-, or three-line stanzas? Is there a better working definition of precarity than the "refusal of the regularization of time"?

Then again, maybe the body belongs to the sixteenth-century nobleman, and the preemption has been preempted by the form it wants to subvert; maybe the form, even in its most unrecognizable contemporary contortions, is playing out an eons-old identity. The essay, that is, has always been associated with movement. Approximately 447 years ago, Montaigne called the essay a thing that "wanders." In "Night and Moonlight" (1862), Thoreau's moonlit walks supply a metaphor for the limits of human knowledge, mirrored in the roaming structure of the essay; an idea is briefly illumined and then eclipsed as the thinker moseys on. Ernest Rhys in 1913 argued that the essay is the work of "dilute lyricists, engaged in pursuing a rhythm too subtle for verse." In 1925 William Carlos Williams called it "pure motion," and Kenneth Burke, in 1941, a "kind of Hamletic soliloquy, its rhythm slowed down to a snail's pace, or perhaps to an irregular jog." The "AI algorithms and content-wallahs and social media provocateurs" not only have "style, character, oomph!"; the essay has—has always had—everything that will come to characterize content.

When reading a hybrid essay, perhaps this is ultimately what bothers me: the endless innovation of optimized content. Anticipating the writer's anticipation of my anticipation, I brace for a scattershot rhythm. Reading is a process of preempting the next move; I read as one might walk down stairs in the dark. The arrhythmia of excitement, of tangents and novelty, undercuts its own force through repetition. When the surprise comes, I am already tired of and by it (Ngai calls this coupling of astonishment and boredom "stuplimity"). This is partly what makes something zany: that it fails to produce the response, usually approval or enjoyment, it is trying with all its might to produce.

This dynamic plays out not just in individual essays. Zoom out and you notice the waves breaking rapidly online, depositing the day's detritus at your feet. If the essay began as a conversation with a dead friend, it carries on now as an argument with vigilant strangers; there is always an imagined interlocutor, thousands of interlocutors, and their intentions are unclear. Exhaustion shadows paranoia and hyperactivity, both for the zany agent and the audience to its zaniness: an affect that indexes the conditions of contemporary production as an exhaustive and exhausting state.

*

We are seeing, more and more, the uncanny-valley effect of writing that functions both as literature and as content — or, more accurately, writing that happens before the bifurcation of these categories. I have one final example in mind, this one published on *BuzzFeedNews*, *BuzzFeed*'s arm for serious journalism: an essay by a young American writer named Shannon Keating. The essay, titled "The Time I Went on a Lesbian Cruise and It Blew Up My Entire Life," is a lengthy meditation on contemporary queer politics filtered through the story of a whirlwind cruise-ship romance that ended her long-term relationship back home. It went viral, continued trending for many months, and (according to Keating) fans of the essay still stop Keating and her new partner in the street to ask after their relationship. It was also featured on *Longform* under the name "Going Overboard," demonstrating its optimization both ways: for

Longform's more neutral aesthetic and for *BuzzFeed*'s ruthlessly zany one.

A few months later, Keating published a piece responding to the cruise ship essay's viral fame, also on *BuzzFeedNews*. This one was published under the title "Writers Want to Be Read. But Do They Want to Be Brands?" Here, Keating reflects on the commodification of identity in the first-person-industrial-complex of memoirs and influencers, venturing a feminist defense of first-person writing even as she worries over the exchange of women's private lives, including her own, for clicks. Three days later, when I checked back, it had assumed the altogether more personal and, well, clickable, title "Am I Writing About My Life, or Selling Myself Out?" It also has a third title — "Caroline Vs. Natalie and My Personal Essay Identity Crisis" — that appears in the results only if you Google "Caroline Vs. Natalie," a cash-in on influencer Caroline Calloway's highly public feud with her ex-ghostwriter, Natalie Beach.

As a senior staff writer and the LGBT editor for *BuzzFeed News*, Keating must have known, even hoped, that her own essay might be sucked into the system she helped create; indeed, in "Writers Want to Be Read," she spends several memoir-y paragraphs discussing her formative years selling memoir online. But she never fully acknowledges her own hefty part in the ploy (say what you will, but you can't reproach this essay for being irreproachable), dodging a mea culpa re: careerism and offering yet another personal revelation in its place: she published the first essay partly to feel better about leaving her partner for her cruise-ship fling.

This is *beside* the point: whatever Keating says or doesn't say in this piece is, mostly, beside the point. Published on the same platform as the cruise essay, it contains hyperlinks to her previous work for *BuzzFeed*, including the cruise essay, as well as a memoir whose "nearly half a million views" she claims to feel "torturously conflicted about" for its participation in the trauma economy. Like all other long-form content on *BuzzFeed*, the essay is primed for scanning in bite-sized paragraphs and sections, its reading experience telegraphed in advance. It is littered (stuffed?) with of-the-moment pop-culture references and Internet parlance. It wears its Tweet/Share/Copy buttons in the same place as usual: after the title and byline but before the article proper. It starts with a personal anecdote before moving on to the premise of the piece. It ends and cedes the floor to a never-ending grid of *BuzzFeed* clickbait. It reproduces the conditions that produced Keating's virality while denouncing them. It knows that this denunciation means next to nothing given that the essay isn't meant to be read, just engaged with, and that engagement can take many forms besides reading. It puts new batteries in the same old machine and expects different results.

Like many essays on the essay—like Geordie Williamson's, which, after all, exists both as part of the anthology and as marketing for the anthology—it functions as a native advertisement for the essay: it is content that mimics the form of the essay precisely. Even as it insists on its prestige, it wants, ultimately, to be consumed, and replicates the conditions that make its production and consumption most efficient. The innovations of hybridity replicate the European essay in its most traditional form, and we see that innovation is, as often as not, a form that preserves and reproduces tradition (the division of wealth, of labor, of genre, of attention) while pretending to annul it. As long as it operates within these conditions, the hybrid essay is structurally unable to fulfill its own brief of transgression. To protect prestige, you need a boundary, and to protect a boundary, you have to be paranoid.

Crypto Forever

On her latest album, in a love song addressed to her sister's baby, the American musician Lana Del Rey sings: "You name your babe Lilac Heaven/After your iPhone 11/'crypto forever'/ screams your stupid boyfriend/Fuck you Kevin." We will refer to the average cryptocurrency investor as Kevin.

Like Smiths fans or Reddit users, the average cryptocurrency investor is assumed to be white, male, and socially maladjusted. The data tends to bear this out. In Australia, the average investor is statistically most likely to live in Brisbane, so let's place Kevin in Brisbane, perhaps in Toowong or Wavell Heights. He is Caucasian, thirty-five years old, with a live-in partner and young child. He invests in seventeen different cryptocurrencies. In the last financial year, he received a modest but healthy return of $12,428 on his investments. He works full-time. He thinks crypto is the future of finance and has a high level of financial literacy. I picture him picnicking at New Farm Park, buying packaged T-shirts at Uniqlo, getting away on the weekends. Maybe if he drank enough IPAs at a games night he *would* scream "crypto forever!"

The average investor is built in the image of the exceptional investor, like a vassal and his lord. The exceptional investor occurs on a spectrum of social maladjustment, perceived or real, from freak, to geek, to businessman. At one end of the spectrum is Brock Pierce (freak), a 5'3" crypto-billionaire former child-star cut from the same swashbuckling cloth as late-career Johnny Depp, right down to the rape allegations. Vitalek Buterin (geek) developed the world's second biggest cryptocurrency, Ethereum, when he was twenty years old, and wears T-shirts printed with cats beaming out rainbow lasers from their eyes. Craig Wright, an ex-Brisbane boy who claims he is Satoshi Nakomoto, the creator of Bitcoin, presents as a businessman in blue checkered shirts and ties. Being exceptional, the exceptional investor operates at the outermost reaches of intensity, is the total fulfillment of his type. He gets profiled in *Rolling Stone*. He gives TED talks and marries models and guests on podcasts. The average investor generally coheres to one of the freak, geek, or businessman archetypes too, but merely as its faint imprint. Every Kevin's goal is to make the leap from average to exceptional.

THE LANA ARCHETYPE

By this point in time, you have probably met plenty of Kevins. Maybe you've had an unprepossessing date with one, maybe your sister married one, maybe he's in your philosophy class. Kevin is probably who you think of when you think of crypto people. Kevins get all the air time, and under the purview of the Kevin archetype, crypto begins to take on Kevin-like qualities—is seen as boring, and geeky, and irredeemably male. In fact, the association of crypto with these qualities is so strong that when a man starts to talk about crypto—no matter how amiable and clear-headed he has seemed up until this point—he instantly becomes a Kevin.

But Kevin should not be charged with telling the full story of crypto. I think that Kevins' hold on the crypto imaginary has become too great. When I look around my own life at the crypto people I know, I see a few Kevins, but many more belonging to a category that we could call the Lana archetype: dreamy artists and poets, engaged in painstaking, mysterious labors and all-consuming romances. There is no hard data on Lana; a Lana would never voluntarily fill out a survey, unless it was for money. But here's what I know from observation and anecdote. Lana is pushing thirty and clings to the underside of the economy. She does not have what you could call a legitimate job, does not own property, and has never married. Her knowledge of financial markets is patchy, though oddly comprehensive when it comes to crypto, about which she has many theories and speculations. She has been in higher arts education for years and is used to dealing in abstractions. The immaterial nature of crypto appeals to her sensibilities; she screams "to the moon!" when drunk on mimosas. I wouldn't want to hang out with Kevin but I have all the time in the world for Lana; I swipe left on Kevins but right on Lanas.

ARE YOU CRYPTO-CURIOUS?

The biggest demographic of the "crypto-curious" in Australia is women. The crypto-curious is someone who does not yet invest or is interested in learning more.

I went with a friend to a crypto information session early last year. The room was full of all kinds of people: a huge guy with a ponytail, dressed all in black; an elderly Chinese woman; several nervy young men; a few middle-aged Anglo-Aussie women. Running the session was an alpha-Kevin and his two female beta-Kevins. The alpha-Kevin spoke in front of a projector screen, while the betas handed out business cards and grinned hugely at my friend and me when we took one.

So not all Kevins are men. And despite the namesake, not all Lanas are women, or white, or heterosexual. Some are gender-queer, some are men. One of the Lanas I know has a poodle and works as a stripper. Another is a Vietnamese-Australian philosopher. Still another is a white, gay fashion curator and writer.

I decided to document a sample group of Lanas. In choosing my subjects, the criteria was simple. They had to have crypto. They had to all know each other. They had to be artists or writers of some kind. And they had to, at least a little bit, want to be famous.

ON THE STRIP

Jeff has a Madonna gap and cherubic blond curls. He comes strolling up to Kat and me just as Kat is putting my big toe in their mouth. We are on the median strip outside a café, basking in the improbable sun and still, warm air. Jeff had told us he needed to shower before leaving the house as he hadn't done it in three days. He said he would be there in about half an hour. That was two hours ago. Boredom and squirmy impatience drove us to the foot thing.

"WHAT IS THIS FOOT FETISH LESBIAN SHIT!" he yells as he approaches.

The twenty-odd fellow baskers turn around to stare.

He settles down beside us and apologizes for not being able to give us a chic European cheek kiss, his usual greeting — not because of Covid, of course, which is still running rampant, but because his face is slick with sunscreen (he's on Retinol). He shrugs off his bag, a green Woolworths one, which I notice is labeled meticulously in small capital letters: JEFFREY L. I remind him this is for my book.

"In that case, open with: "Jeff, an incredibly swole, handsome, EARLY man...""

Jeff, Kat says later, is in a great mood today. When he's in a mood like this, his gregariousness cannot be contained by mere good humor and kindness; it expands into baser modes of expression, like slurs and insults, and transforms them into a riotous kind of affection. Kat had advocated strongly for dawdling on the way to meet Jeff.

"You'll see," they said.

Kat knows what he's like. They have been friends for about five years now. When Jeff meets someone he wants to befriend, Kat says, he is very intense about it. He is, in general, obsessed with people. "That person is *amazing*," he will say about a perfectly normal-seeming stranger or acquaintance, and then you see it too — how great that person really is. Kat was one of those people for Jeff. They met through mutual friends after Jeff moved back to Melbourne from New York (an origin story involving a guy from Grindr, a dinner party, and several invented personae) and then they started going out together on weekends, and then sleeping over at each other's houses, and then three days would pass and they would still be hanging out, and then they'd meet up a couple days later to debrief about it all.

I had known Jeff peripherally for a few years when he pitched me as a romantic prospect to Kat. He did this without me knowing about it, a true act of altruism, especially given that one of our first conversations had culminated in me insulting him. ("Is that Comme Tees?," he asked, gesturing at my shirt. I replied that I didn't really care about fashion. I later discovered that he curated fashion shows, wrote about fashion, and studied fashion at university, i.e., that he cared about fashion a lot.) Kat and I ran into Jeff on our second date, a few meters farther up from where we are now, on a patch of grass hallowed by the full bottle of natural wine that slowly trickled from the bottom of Kat's tote bag into the soil. That afternoon, Kat and I talked a lot about crypto. Jeff, Kat, and I are all, to different extents and in the full sense of the word, invested in crypto, Jeff most of all.

According to Jeff, crypto is: "a space for degens" (degenerates), "mostly vaporwave," "a bit Drain Gang," "literally immaterial," "a Ponzi scheme," "a bubble," "sort of Alt-right," and "an umbrella term for blockchain technology."

"Honestly," he says. "I'm such a midwit, I really don't know what it is. I have maybe one IQ point more than other people who are into it."

Jeff cares less about what crypto is and more about what it can do for him. He is now in the final months of his PhD on fashion curating. His scholarship has run out and he is using crypto to try and replace his meager Centrelink payments. He makes most money from day-trading crypto, which he has been doing for about a year. Day-trading is when you buy and sell assets over a short time frame, i.e., a day, making money incrementally as you go. You buy when the price is low and — hopefully — sell when high, and repeat. Jeff has about twenty different coins and alarms set at different support prices (you buy at support and sell at resistance). He always does it on his computer, never his phone. He sets his risk-reward parameters in advance, and also sets his take-profit lines, the points at which you sell throughout the day. His first big loss was of nine thousand U.S. dollars, after which he took a break.

"I completely changed my trade thesis," he assures me. "But at the end of the day, it's just numbers on a screen, and you become stronger after it."

He refuses to tell me how much money he has made or how much money he has right now.

Kat is a writer. They released their first book of poetry earlier this year, and are now working on a novel. They also work at a brothel. Writing and fucking: guess which one earns them a living? When they get an influx of money, they like to put some of it in crypto. "I encounter large sums of money that I need to tax evade all the time. But I don't want to keep it in cash. Large amounts don't feel real anyway. And cash doesn't feel real. It's like, cash, what is this object?" Right now, they have $1,086 in their bank account, $17,756 in crypto, and "some more on the way..."

Kat first got into crypto nine years ago, when they bought

$500 of Bitcoin Cash on the advice of a fellow sex worker. Actually, it turned out they had been told to buy Bitcoin, but bought Cash by accident. If you look at a comparison chart, Bitcoin's line is a rocky but precipitous incline, Everest, while Bitcoin Cash is a walk in the park along a spirit level. The distance between Bitcoin and Bitcoin Cash's highest peaks is, on my laptop screen, a hand's width apart.

Jeff interjects. "No fucking way. If you had bought nine years ago, you would have been one of the *ear*liest adopters."

"Yeah. I bought $500."

"Uh-uh."

"It's different when you do sex work. Sex workers were way ahead of the game."

Jeff checks his phone. "Bitcoin Cash was only invented in 2017."

"Whatever. You know I'm bad at math."

Jeff says that Kat should withdraw all their money from the bank and keep it somewhere that pays higher interest. He says phrases like: "margin call," "bear cave," "macro." He says, "If you're bullish crypto macro." He says, "local bottom," but it has nothing to do with a location-based sex-app. Kat wants to know where they should put their savings.

Jeff rolls his eyes and says, "DYOR."

"What?"

"Do Your Own Research."

We pause for a moment as two butch lesbians walk by with a cat in a stroller. I ask Kat and Jeff why so many of our friends are into crypto when most of them have so little money.

"It's weird," Kat agrees. "Most of the people I know who are into it are unemployed."

They think this has to do with the system being so transparently unfair. Melbourne is full of young, bourgeois leftists who don't like talking about money and who would never touch crypto—for environmental reasons, for ethical reasons—but who are set to inherit multimillion-dollar properties from their families. Crypto represents a shortcut for people who would otherwise need to work decades to even afford a down payment. And when your weekly paycheck comes in well below the poverty line, blowing it all on a risky investment feels relatively low-stakes; it would feel much worse to try to diligently squirrel it away.

Jeff checks his phone and hooks his green bag over his arm—he has to go and meet up with a friend with whom he's putting together an arts grant. We walk up the street, and as we approach a sprawling and nondescript megacafé, he turns to Kat and me and speaks in a hushed, fervent voice.

"You know this place? I went here the other day and they have this thing called the breakfast pocket, which is really yummy, like bacon and egg, for really cheap. So I asked for a breakfast pocket but the waiter was like, 'I don't know what you're talking about.' He denied that he'd ever heard of the breakfast pocket, even though it's listed right there on the menu. Then I described it, and he was like, 'oh you mean the *breakfast wrap*.' Then I went back the next day and made sure I got a different waiter, and I ordered 'the breakfast pocket' again, and the waiter was again like, 'we don't have that.' And then I went back a *third* time and got a new waiter, and she also denied knowing about the pocket. *But she was smirking as she said it.*"

Sunscreen or no, he kisses us both goodbye.

AT VINCE'S HOUSE

When I arrive, Vince says, in a tone of deep suspicion, "I was speaking to Jeff earlier today, and he said the interview was pretty chill."

Vince lives in a sharehouse in a two-story terrace with a courtyard. His entire house, including the bedrooms, is carpeted in bright red floral carpet, thick underfoot. The toilet is behind slatted cupboard doors next to the kitchen and looks exactly like a pantry from the outside. Vince's own room is more nondescript than I'd imagined. It could not be picked out of a lineup of Melbourne art student bedrooms. He has a tiny, slender laptop, a desk beneath a window crammed with green foliage, a mantelpiece of books—I had thought there would be more books—an unmade double bed, empty cups. It's messy, but not notably so. It looks like some work happens here, but in a dilettante's way. You might assume from the state of this room that its occupant is an unserious bachelor, but you would be wrong; Vince is writing two books, finishing his PhD, partying for up to forty-eight hours at a time, and is ruinously in love.

Jeff and Kat think Vince is a hopeless romantic. The term they use to describe his attitude toward crypto is "hopeium."

On the strip, earlier that day, Kat says, "He's hopeium about everything in his life."

Jeff says, "Vince is such a product of market psychology."

In the courtyard, Vince says, "When I'm reading dry, economic texts, it's like porn, better than porn in fact, because I don't really like porn. I've only ever watched porn for educational purposes."

Vince is perhaps the only person who could say this and I'd believe it. In the last three months, he has read all three volumes of *Capital*, Friedrich Hayek's main works, and Adam Smith's *The Wealth of Nations*. Whenever he talks about philosophy or economics, his eyes are alight with genuine rapture; ditto when he talks about love. He is by himself for half of the week, and the other half he spends with his girlfriend Lois. He and Lois are "in the throes of sublime early romance." Together, they make TikToks, go to parties, and watch reality TV shows like *FBOY Island*. When he's on his own, he wakes up around nine or ten and reads and writes until evening.

"Annihilating romance, dry economic theory, and no porn," is Vince's summary.

To understand his relationship to one, you have to understand his relationship to all. His worldview is gorgeously consistent. He has figured out a philosophy of perfect harmony in which love, money, partying, and the likely trajectory of world history all circle a central axis. Descartes needed the self to make his grand unified theory of knowledge work. Marx, the labor theory of value. For the secular man, the axis might be family. For Vince, as far as I can tell, it's "competitive dynamics." He thinks all aspects of life should be submitted to competition, similar to what happens in a free market, where products and services are produced, optimized, and culled as actors compete to produce the best and cheapest goods. He thinks that to remain competitive, manufacturers and corporations must advance technology and so, the market produces technological innovation. He thinks that the way the market makes decisions—through an automated, decentralized process—is a better model for rational thought than anything humans can manage. He thinks, therefore, that humans should do everything they can to surrender to the market. It should not be stopped. It should not be bargained with. And anyway, it already won, a couple of hundred years ago. World history since then is just an arbitration of the details.

"Capitalism was Skynet," Vince says. "The Industrial Revolution was the singularity—the moment when we accidentally created an artificial superintelligence that's escaped, and now is the only political actor, the only thing with agency, and we're just living inside it, like little cogs and wheels."

In this view of economics, crypto is the automaton's next leap forward. Crypto is Vince's vision of full competition, full decentralization, and full automation in practice. Around the monoculture of the U.S. dollar, a thousand cryptocurrencies bloom. They spring up and die out, and while some, like Bitcoin, are perennial, they are always at risk from scrappy newcomers. Some blockchains can host smart contracts, which automatically execute agreements without them ever having to pass through a lawyer's hands. The blockchain also paved the way for NFTs, which are a way of owning — and proving that you own — digital assets, and which are almost always purchased with crypto. For all this, Vince only bought in late in the game, early in 2021.

"You and Kat were invested way before me. I remember being at that dinner at yours, me and Annabelle were like, 'dammit!' Cause you guys were so happy that day."

"We were in love and becoming rich. What more could you ask for?"

"We were out of love and becoming poor."

They broke up the same night, beginning the process while waiting for the Uber outside my door. In the following weeks and months, Vince poured more and more of his money into crypto. He might once have used drugs to ease his heartache; investing felt like the healthier choice for a party-hardened almost-thirty-year-old, and it had the same exhilarating effects. He relished crypto's volatility. When the value of a coin soared or crashed, in peak moments of euphoria and despair, he felt it in his body as strong as any drug.

Now the effects have worn off a little, now he's back in love,

Vince wants from crypto what most people want. Like Jeff, Vince is using crypto to try and replace his vanishing income. He hopes crypto will allow him to continue his current lifestyle of reading and writing after his PhD scholarship ends ("hopefully I'll just never have to get a real job"). He doesn't day-trade because it would be too disruptive to his routine. He just holds. When I ask how much he has, he says that it's highly classified information, that he only talks in percentages (around 10 percent of everything he has is in crypto), and that there are a lot of rumors flying around about his finances, all of them untrue. He once told Jeff the real amount when they were both drunk, but Jeff can't remember it.

"Anyway, isn't it generally considered rude to ask ...?"

Vince's background is "kind of poor." His father comes from "a literal peasant family in Vietnam," and his mother, a white Australian, was a violinist in the Adelaide Symphony Orchestra. "My dad was a boat person, and my mum was doing refugee work. *Apocalypse Now* had to happen for me to exist." His mum retired from playing violin after developing Parkinson's, and his dad, who physically deteriorated from years of working as a laborer, no longer works either. They are both on pensions. His sister is a Liberal-voting corporate lawyer who lives in Sydney and helps them out with money. He says he used to fight with her a lot because he disagreed with her politics, but now —

Jeff says, "When I first met Vince he was kind of a socialist and now he's like [self-important voice]: 'the right wing win again!'"

I remember this too. I don't fully recall how Vince and I met, but I remember it was around the time he was dating my friend, a dyed-in-the-wool socialist. A few months after their amicable but definitive split, they took opposite sides in an organized debate at the 2020 Marxism Conference — topic: "Nihilistic Communism vs Anti-Nihilistic Communism." Vince took the side of nihilism.

"I was a hardcore Marxist and Leninist," Vince explains. "This was about ten years ago, when I lived in Adelaide, and I was in Socialist Alternative for a couple of years. But I always did what I wanted, I didn't always follow the rules. And I had a real soft spot for Maoism and they really hated that. Then in late 2019 — I was in Melbourne at this point — I finally abandoned any kind of Marxist, leftist politics. This was all mediated by philosophy, so the continuous commitment to critique — what is the most radical gesture? Back then I thought that was communist revolution, but now I think that's just way too human. A communist revolution looks revolutionary if the outer reaches of reality are the human as opposed to, like, situating the human in a cosmic timeline where it's just some random species. So that's why I made my great betrayal, I guess. It was actually *really* painful. I felt really sad, I kept doing these random bets to myself, like, 'if Bernie Sanders and Jeremy Corbyn both lose,' cause I was totally sure they would win, 'I'll renounce any kind of leftism...' Corbyn lost, and then it was all down to Bernie, then Bernie lost. It was an actual breakup."

Pause.

"It's not that I'm *for* capitalism. It's only when I'm in philosophical mode, because it's the consummation of critique, it critiques better and harder and faster than philosophy ever could. As a philosopher I'm for it, but as a human, I think it's obviously horrific for humans, but at the same time it can't be stopped. And philosophically nor should it be stopped."

I ask, "Does the philosopher come into conflict with the human?"

"I've been making a conscious attempt to collapse theory and praxis. It's becoming easier and easier...What does Garret say in *FBOY Island*? He's like, 70 percent F boy, 30 percent nice guy by the end. I'd say I'm 70 percent philosopher, 30 percent human anyway so it was already pretty easy to ignore the 30 percent. It turns out collapsing theory and praxis is amazing, because all it is is latching on to nihilistic processes that mirror what capital is doing, which typically are: raving, love, drugs, partying, aesthetic practices, couture. It's actually been beautiful, it's like therapy in a way: you can love what's happening; you don't have to be horrified by the present anymore, or by some lost future."

While going through his great betrayal—"at the exact same time"—he met Jeff. Jeff became obsessed with Vince, just as he had with Kat a couple years prior. Through Jeff, Vince met Kat "and that whole crew, which I would consider to be—maybe Kat less so—in a positive sense, vastly more politically nihilistic than anything I had encountered before. And that was really attractive. I don't really talk about philosophy with any of them, hardly ever, but there's something about it...they're the praxis.

They are practicing the concepts of—they're going to raves, kick-ons, making art, curating fashion shows. If you think that capital is revolutionary, revolutionary praxis doesn't become something like, red flags, it becomes making TikToks, swiping on Tinder. That is revolutionary, genuinely I think that's what revolution is: contributing data to the capitalist algorithm. Maybe this is due to personal investment, the fact that everyone I've ever loved, I've met due to slide-ins on Instagram..."

You'd think that love would have no place in Vince's vision of human annihilation. How can love survive competitive dynamics? But Vince sees no opposition between the two. He describes how when he first met his girlfriend during Melbourne's strict Covid lockdowns, they were legally required to quarantine for two weeks. They talked online, and when they saw each other in person it was at a distance. He compares this to courtly love, in which the suitor wins the affection of a lover through a series of codified rituals and deeds that exquisitely delay the coupling. This is a lot like Tinder, which seems to facilitate instant gratification but which is actually a finely tuned system of frustration. Conversations go nowhere; girls swipe right on the lucky few, ignoring the teeming masses. Dating apps submit romance to competition, and for Vince, this is "super romantic. It's like, medieval style, performing deeds in the form of thot pics."

Jeff and Kat are right about Vince; he *is* a hopeless romantic. It's clear, too, that his great betrayal was also the start of a great love, or loves. He returns to talking about Jeff, the months when they first became friends.

"For some reason in that period," Vince says, talking about when he first met Jeff, "partying was really fruitful. There was something beautiful about being deranged, coming down, then Tuesday to Friday manically writing, and then going out for three days, and doing it again, for six whole months. Everything since then has been squeezing the juice from that era when I try to write."

From another perspective, maybe even a mainstream one, love is a low-tech route to human annihilation. So you see why Vince is into love, raving, drugs, and crypto; these are all forms of annihilation. With every crush, every purchase, every double-tap, Vince moves himself closer to his ideal world, the only world that he thinks—that he thinks capital thinks—is viable and desirable. I think that Vince must have the clearest conscience in Melbourne. All that *and* he gets to make a little money on the side.

FLAGSTAFF GARDENS

Ashley starts speaking before I can even start recording. I'm settling us into a patch of grass in the park, unloading plastic tubs of olives and tomatoes and sleeves of cured meats. Her dog, Chomp, a large black curly-haired poodle (purebred) is off leash and gamboling around the park. When I start lifting the lids on containers he returns to us and puts his snout everywhere, slobbering and snuffling. Ashley's gaze remains fixed in the distance, as though she is distracted by a half-remembered thought, while I try to wrangle the dog. This happens continuously throughout the interview, me hanging on to Chomp's collar, Ashley ignoring us both. Imagine this conversation underlaid by the rhythm of heavy dog panting.

"In 2017," she says, "I had this friend who set up this program. You could type in a URL on any computer, and the program would run in the background mining crypto. He would go into shops and libraries and set it up on display computers. He made like ten grand within a month, but I was sort of worried — I've seen people go yellow watching a screen. He wasn't really sleeping, just watching the market. He explained this program to me and that's how I first heard about crypto."

She pauses to accept a glass of sparkling water.

"When I finally invested, years later, it was this really witchy kind of experience. I thought I'd be getting this payment of £10,000 from the UK — for UK rates payers — then I fucked it up, cause I sent them an email saying I'd come to Australia. I was really high on the idea that I'd be getting this random money. I thought, if I get it, I'm going to put it in Tesla. This was in March or April, it was a Capricorn full moon, whatever that month is. And there was a storm, and I have this superstition that you should always make big decisions during a storm.

"Then at midnight my brother calls me, and he *never* calls. He was like, 'I'm in NSW, I just got off the water, I was surfing during a windstorm with sharks — I'm gonna put 10K in Bitcoin.' He said the guys he was with bought Bitcoin before the first bull run, and predicted it was gonna blow up in May. I was stoned — I was like, 'woah.' So these guys are surfers from Sydney, and I was like, if you're gonna trust anyone, if anyone's gonna know how to predict a market it's surfers. Cause they study waves. Every morning they get up and look at charts of the surf. Also, waves are connected to the moon. And you can easily apply that kind of chart reading of patterns to humans, especially men, who act certain ways according to the moon. Then I told Kat and everyone to buy Bitcoin."

Ashley is Kat's godsister. They grew up together, on and off, when they both lived in the same town in regional Victoria. For the whole year Kat and I have been dating, I am pretty sure Ashley has *noticed* me—next to Kat, in their friendship group, in photos of Kat and me—but maybe the impression never solidified into reality. When I make a joke about this being the first ever sister-in-law meetup, meaning her and me, she merely gazes at me in confusion. She is stick thin, with chin-length red hair. Today she is wearing pink sneakers, a pink sweater tied around her shoulders, and a silk scarf trailing from under her cap—a chic legionnaire's hat. She is in her early thirties, is always wearing bug-eyed Anna Wintour sunglasses, and thought she was an alcoholic for about a year, but now doesn't, and so along with the small goods I've also bought her champagne, because Kat says she loves it when anyone encourages her to drink after so many tiptoes around the matter. She works at a strip club in the city and lives in an apartment adjoining an art gallery, which has running water but no shower or bath. She has just Met Someone, and jokes about sending him to take his romantic post-coital shower at the gym she's a member of, where she uses the change rooms for her toilette.

Like any good artist/eccentric, Ashley has a strict daily routine. Every day, she either "wakes up really early or really late," takes Chomp to Royal Park first thing, and rollerblades around the grass circle five times. She returns home to drink coffee, reply to her messages, and clean her apartment; she says she cleans her apartment every single day. Then she does some work in her studio, designing and making clothes. She comes to this park for the dog hour—an hour when dogs are allowed off leash and a designated area fills with rolling, running purebreds. Sometimes she meets up with an older man who also owns a poodle. Then she returns home to make dinner for herself and meditate for "like two hours" to try and get to sleep without her phone. Her screen time averages nine hours a day, or as she puts it: "I spend all day on my phone talking to women with BPD on Instagram."

"And then the weekend is what I'd describe as clinical partying," she says, referring to her job as a stripper. "Being paid to party."

For a while, as well, she was in what she calls a Christian Twitter crypto cult, which revolved around day-trading, and eventually set up its own coin. Basically, it was a group chat of mostly very young crypto fanatics. Everyone in the group was anonymous. At first, she was into creating the illusion that she was hiding out in Indonesia, wanted for information related to sex trafficking. Eventually she self-doxxed and posted a photo; the zoomers told her how pretty she was for a thirty-one-year-old. The idea was that she would promote the new coin at work to wealthy clients. The coin was set up through Metamask, and collapsed when it got called out for being a pyramid scheme by some big accounts on Twitter, and by some of the investors who lost money on it.

"But everyone ended up losing money on it, so it wasn't really a pyramid scheme, just a bit of a gamble."

Only — Ashley never owned any because she never figured out how to buy it presale, which depressed her.

"I realized my role in the group was more like a cheerleader, which is something that I do at my job but I get paid for that? If I'd been making a bunch of money it would be worth it, but I wasn't. I was actually losing money. And the way that the adrenaline would go up in the group, and everyone would be screaming, 'buy this, buy this!' And I was going through the same emotions with them but I'd never have the right app or platform to buy this or that particular currency. I had this other theory that the dopamine cycle of trading is then even more intense when you're on your own cycle. I would go over my Twitter feed and it would just be a documentation of my menstrual cycle. A PMS diary."

She says that some people in the group got rich, but the trade-off was being online "literally every moment they were awake." If they weren't trading, they were on Twitter. If they weren't on Twitter, they were in the group chat. Intragroup romances were common. She says that because most of them were Christian, they had strict ideals around sex. They believed you should only court someone with a view to marriage, but because their relationships were entirely virtual, no one ever got married.

"Which is kind of the way they would engage with money," Ashley says. "This eternal striving for more and more, but not taking any out to live in the now or reap the benefits."

As for Ashley, she pulled out some of her crypto to buy Chomp.

"Sometimes I feel weird that I have this designer dog and I'm broke, but... people who have been in investment for a long time all say you have to invest in yourself first."

At this point, the designer dog in question, who has been sprinting around the park in widening loops, approaches a man who is dandling a small baby, lowering its bare kicking feet onto the grass, and enthusiastically snuffles its stomach. The man plucks the baby up and leaps backward, yelling, "Fuck off! Fuck off!" He looks around in the outraged self-consciousness of the publicly wronged, but his gaze skims past us. Chomp continues his loops. Ashley continues talking, unfazed.

"During the crypto run this year, it was probably the best three months I had in Australia in a strip club, ever. There is a financial calendar of strip clubs but they usually revolve more around events: AFL, Grand Prix, and so on. I don't think many girls realized there were all these random new millionaires who were incels and wanted to have a lap dance. Guys would come in and show you their portfolio and you'd be like, 'Ooh tell me more!' And they're like, 'You wouldn't understand.' I think I've personally made more money trading stocks and that's cause it's not so gatekept, people actually just wanna share information. I think women are better trend forecasters, so it doesn't make sense why they're being excluded. These men who were actually kind of losers, sure they might have a few degrees but they've never really gotten a job, they've suddenly got all this money, and it means they can get chicks, and then they can have her in a patriarchal position where she doesn't know how to make any money herself and, take care of the home I guess? I think the whole trad culture was like that. Maybe Red Scare kind of started it. I guess that needed to happen cause we were in a bleak era of chaotic polyamory and sex addiction but, I dunno, I have had arguments with these kinds of crypto characters. They're like, 'how are you not married and you're thirty-one? And you work in a strip club?' "

Chomp is now playing with a tiny dog that belongs to two pale young men in ill-fitting black clothes, who are both drinking Mothers. I wince every time Chomp and the dog tussle, but neither the dog nor its owners seem to mind. It strikes me that these two could well be Kevins of the geek variety, just the kind of guy that Ashley is describing, at least cosmetically. The small dog yelps and Chomp moves on to a girl reading alone on a picnic blanket, who strokes his head with real enthusiasm.

"I feel like I've experienced classism from people that don't even realize they're doing it. There was a period, whenever I complained about being depressed or whatever, people would tell me to get a different job. Maybe that's whorephobia but I don't think it was, it was like, you should be doing something more with your life. I had the same comments when I was in hospitality as well. Even though Covid happens and the only people who have secure work are like baristas and people who work in supermarkets. Crypto's played a role as well. Some of my friends have come into this money and have started having certain standards that are new. I know some people who are completely sold on the politics of crypto. They really believe it's gonna be the future. But all I've seen is a bunch of people who wouldn't necessarily become capitalist become capitalist."

There's a shriek. The man with the baby lifts it above his head. Chomp is springing up and down around the man, barking gleefully.

"Fuck OFF!"

Ashley at last whistles for Chomp. The man marches toward us.

"Is this your dog? I've reported him to the council. I thought he was a stray."

"Well, he's wearing a collar."

"He's attacking us!"

Ashley rolls her eyes, and says to me in an undertone, "They've already fined me once."

Chomp bounds up to Ashley and Ashley clips a leash onto his rhinestone-studded collar. We collect our possessions and start walking. The man is rooted to the spot by befuddled rage. We walk in silence for a moment or two. She returns to the subject of her new lover.

"So...I guess I have a boyfriend now. It's really random."

People Who Lunch

Everyone has told me I should talk to Willem. Willem is rumored to have made a fortune on NFTs. Willem has a big following on Twitter. Willem (I hear) has just cut off his waist-length blond hair. Willem (I heard this quite recently) has sworn to never let crypto rule his life again. When Willem closes his eyes, he sees the afterburn of blue light.

Willem lives in Jeff's old house (by the time of our conversation, Jeff has moved back to New York), on a street full of tall, narrow terraces. I arrive a little after 8 p.m. and Nicole answers the door wearing a pink singlet and no bra, halfway through a cigarette. She goes upstairs to fetch Willem and I go to wait in the lounge room.

This house is notorious for being a party house. Glamorous canapés and champagne house; scary kick-ons house; cigarette butts ground into cheese-board house; illegal parties during lockdown house; dress-up dinner party house—all of these things at different times, and sometimes all in the same twenty-four-hour period. I was wondering about moving in here a few months ago. I knew it was the messiest known sharehouse on the millennial circuit, but sometimes I'd go around for a drink, and the sun would be streaming into the back room, hitting the chrome of the replica Le Corbusier sofa just so, and Jeff would be vigorously spray-and-wiping the stove, and I'd think, *maybe*. Tonight, though, the coffee table in the lounge room is crowded with empty beer bottles and two full ashtrays, and the carpet is giving off a dense, organic smell. The kitchen looms behind us as a towering presence, like one huge encrusted pot.

Nicole reappears in the lounge, Willem on her heels.

"Sorry for the dank vibe," she says, giggling.

Willem leaves the room to get a fresh beer and is gone for a long time. When he returns and sits on the couch, I see that the rumors are true: Willem has cut his hair. He is wearing a covetable blue T-shirt of the perfect stretch and softness, turned inside out so that the rough edges of the collar and sleeves are showing (I have known a lot of people who are very into the Internet, and all of them, at least some of the time, wear their T-shirts inside out), rumpled white pants that have been cut off, jaggedly, above the knees, clean white socks, and tennis shoes. His hair is now chin-length and brown. Nicole wanders in and out of the room while Willem and I talk, sitting down, rolling a cigarette, going upstairs, coming back down. She wants to know who I've talked to so far.

"Ashley was telling me the story of how she bought crypto —," I say.

Nicole interjects — "Something about a storm?"

Willem, "And surfing?"

Nicole, "Yeah, I've heard that story before."

Willem studied graphic design, and now does the occasional freelance job in tech and design. Mostly though, thanks to his success in crypto and NFTs, he is able to focus on making art: typically video and digital works, things he will present as NFTs. When I ask him what his life looks like day-to-day, he offers a series of vague propositions and ends by saying, "Um, it's just like...I try to set my life up so I can do things the way I wanna do them. It's seriously just like any freelancer, really."

Everyone told me I should talk to Willem. Everyone also told me that Willem is very private and might not want to talk to me. I think Willem picked a middle road: talk to me but keep it strictly business. Talking to Willem is like drinking a glass of room-temperature water, refreshing and unfussy. Where the others all speak either fast and loud, or fast and a lot, with the fervor of visionaries, he talks at a regular pace at a regular volume. He says the word "space" a lot; ditto with the word "outcome." If he has any unreasonable views, his privacy holds them back, and he therefore comes across as extremely reasonable. When I ask why he first bought crypto, he says, simply: "It seemed like a really obvious hedge to make." When I ask him to explain what crypto is, he says: "It's just a decentralized ledger-based financial asset." When I ask why all the artists we know are into crypto, he says, "Cause they need to make money, I guess." Willem is so reasonable that when I leave his house, approximately two hours later, I am thinking thoughts like, "I need to get into Web3," and "Maybe capitalism does work."

Willem first started buying crypto in 2016. He rode the bull market of 2016-17 all the way up and all the way back down again. Then, he says, he forgot about it as the market became bearish, and only got back into it during the pandemic. Willem worked on the same coin as Ashley; he did the branding, which takes its cues from *Scarface*, all neon pink and deep ocean blue, convertibles, palm trees, private jets.

Ashley: "I was always saying that my character at work was Michelle Pfeiffer in *Scarface*. When I worked in London I'd wear gowns, and I had her hair. And I carried that on in Melbourne and everyone was like, 'Um what is this vibe, wear a bikini.'"

The coin, Willem tells me, was not a scam. It was just a shitcoin.

"The market took a crash. If you look in the founder's wallets, they didn't take any money from it at all."

To make money in crypto, Willem says, you have to be able to endure multiple losses. And to be a really good trader, it's a cliché in the business that you have to leave your emotions out of it.

"There was a point in time when I had a really good win on one of these shitcoins, and I made like a 40× profit." He pronounces "×" like "ex." "And then," he continues, "I had all this money, and I started leverage trading. Which is like, you can basically trade with more money than you have."

"Like what the banks do," I say.

"Yeah. So you can be like, 'I'm gonna enter this position with 10X leverage, 30X leverage,' and they'll basically give you a loan for the remaining amount. But it means if the price goes down you can get liquidated really quickly, because you don't have the margin to cover it. So you either long or short it, either hoping it'll go up or down, and if it goes the right way you can make so much money, really, really quickly. I was like 'Woah, I can enter these trades and make a week's salary in two minutes.' But it was just straight gambling. And then I got cocky, and I lost—The market crashed, had a kind of flash dump, every position I had got liquidated."

"How much money did you lose?"

Long pause, awkward laughter.

"You don't have to say," I say.

"Yeah, I prefer not to say," he says.

For the last year or so, Willem has moved away from trading crypto and instead gotten deep in the NFT "space." I ask Willem to explain NFTs, and he pauses before offering: "a trustless form of ownership." He has been buying, selling, trading, and making NFTs. He is also working in Web3, on which, more later. Web3, crypto, NFTS. Maybe you have spent your adult life resisting being too online, periodically detoxing from social media, gaming moderately or not at all. Your passing familiarity with these terms has been underscored by disbelief or contempt, you managed to block out the whole Game Stop thing, you learned about NFTs along with everyone else and thought them stupid, only to find that now—in early 2022—these are the ingredients for a whole new future.

"The narrative right now," says Willem, is "GameFi everything."

GameFi: gaming and finance together at last. Though NFTs first blew up in the art world, they make most sense in a world that is already digital. The natural next step, then, is to put them in video games. Gamers already buy items inside games, the most popular of these being guns and skins. Made into NFTs, your character's skin (appearance) and guns could be totally unique, not shared with any other player. Or, players might compete to finish a campaign first, vying for the prize of a rare NFT attribute which could then be traded or sold for serious real-world money.

"If you're in a third-world country you can earn a living wage playing these games," Willem says.

"Which is kind of dark, right?" I say.

"Well, these people are going to be laboring away in a game world, but they have no access to...They can't make a living wage at all, but they can at least play this game and make a living. But I feel like the idea of anyone having to live their life inside a virtual world, even Zoom, that's not a desirable outcome."

The thing about NFTs and gaming is that what happens in-game is not going to stay in-game. For example: Nike just started selling real sneakers paired with NFT versions of the same shoe, which, in a future iteration of the Internet that runs off the blockchain (this is what Web3 is, a blockchain Internet), can be worn by your avatar. Outside of games, Willem tells me, people are eagerly buying artworks that can be used as profile pictures: humanoid cartoon apes and dogs, anime girls, CGI likenesses of themselves. In the future, you can imagine people buying and customizing NFT avatars that walk and talk in the metaverse. These avatars will need clothes and accessories, maybe even housing. You might own two houses—one in the metaverse and one in the material world. You could get to be rich in two worlds or poor in both. You will be playing The Sims of your own life, sans cheat codes.

"The way I read that is that they've just run out of things to sell in the real world. You know, like we're up to iPhone 13, and there's thirty models of Jordans out there. They just can't keep making new things. It's a way to be like, 'Hey, now you can buy a digital pair of shoes, or digital land'..."

This is what companies like Meta, formerly Facebook, want for the future of the Internet. It's pretty much the opposite of what Willem wants. He wants to get back to basics, to the early days of computing, with devices that "can't hijack your monkey brain and get you addicted to apps." He imagines something "stripped back, lightweight," like Kindle, for instance: a simple e-ink display with limited functions.

He takes a similarly moderate approach to NFTs. In fact, he thinks the biggest thing wrong with the NFT space is how excessive it is. The people inside the space have a vested interest in hyping up their projects, even when the art is (Willem's words) "lowest common denominator vibes." Meanwhile, those who could apply a critical eye to the works being made either don't understand NFTs or think the whole medium is irredeemably bad, politically and aesthetically.

"You can see it, there's this really funny thing—there's generally been a sentiment of 'NFTs are cringe, they're bad for the environment.' Then in the NFT space, the sentiment is that the traditional art world is stifled and cringe, and that we're the cool online radicals."

Willem wants to solve this impasse with — wait for it — critics. He wants to see critics who are across both worlds, without vested interest in either, and who can hold both to account. Critics can check the hopeium tendencies of NFT diehards. They can prune the space of non-starters and elevate good work. In doing so, they can also intervene in the market, popping bubbles inflated by arbitrary hype.

"Having critics be able to give things a canonical context allows people to speculate on their value a little bit more accurately."

I take this to mean that Willem wants goalposts so he can bet on who's going to score the winning goal. I'm flattered, in spite of myself, imagining critics as main characters in the story of capitalism, not just taste-makers but market-makers...

When I see Willem at Ashley's fashion show a few weeks later, he looks like the boyfriend you could have in the stripped-back metaverse, wearing sneakers that look like NFTs and a worn-in leather motorcycle jacket. The things Willem believes in for the future are things that already exist or have existed at one time in the past — a minimalist Internet, the blockchain — making it easy to trust his foresight. He believes in capitalism, but not in the way Vince believes in capitalism. He believes in it simply, easily, without any of Vince's sci-fi world-building. Where Vince sees capital as the motor of tech supremacy, Willem's ideology is bolstered by something more traditional. And this is perhaps the only unbelievable thing about Willem (though it makes sense when you think about it) — the fact that he is a Christian.

"It's like, uh, Jesus is the answer. I don't think Bitcoin is the answer to anything. It's just a tool. It has to be moral."

When he first started investing, he quickly learned that single-mindedly pursuing wealth was "deeply unsatisfying." Now he wants to make money, sure, but only so he can opt out of a system where "you're gonna be crushed by everything." He is not talking about a financial system here. He does not mean capitalism. He is talking about the secular world: "the governmental, social bureaucracy that we live under that has its own atheistic morality and its own agenda." His ambitions are modest. "I'm not gonna be able to save the world. I'm not like, 'I can make so much money that I'll save the whole world,' but if you can help yourself, your family, your friends, that seems like a desirable outcome, and that seems feasible at least."

I'm having a strong emotional response that surprises me. When I interview someone, I've observed that I often find myself onside with whoever it is I'm talking to. It's not because I want to extract information that people are more likely to give me if I agree with them (although that's surely part of it), but that I get something out of being inducted into somebody else's worldview. My own investments in crypto have always been minor; I have risked little and lost little, even if I've frequently wanted to be the kind of person who goes all in. Jeff, Kat, Vince, and Ashley are all this kind of person. After each conversation, having emptied myself out in order to receive their answers, I felt, for a few hours afterward, sometimes for a day or two, that I

was occupied by a new mode of being: Jeff and Kat's insouci-
ance, Vince's conviction, Ashley's self-possession. I have been
just as seduced by Willem and his calm pragmatism, but now —
God and family? His comments throw me out of my lulled state
for long enough to register an objection.

"Other people would wanna take a more collective route out
of this quandary..." I say, trailing off. He shrugs. We've reached
an impasse.

I think that Willem is a Lana masquerading as a Kevin. After I
stopped recording and put my phone away, Willem and I had a
long, easygoing, and personal conversation. I know what his parents did before they retired, what kinds of books he reads, and
which American it-girl authors he thinks are talented. He also
told me about how he came to religion. He had first been into
chaos magic, which, at least according to the trend forecasting
think tank K-Hole, whose PDFs we both read in the 2010s, is a
way of bringing something into reality by deciding to believe in
it. Chaos magic, K-Hole writes, is "mixing your own Kool-Aid,
deciding how strong to make it." Willem decided to try out different religions, treating them during the experiment as if he were
already a believer. He decided he would do this until one stuck.
He tried out astrology, Buddhism, Hinduism, Islam, Hermeticism,
Gnosticism, Orthodox Christianity, and Catholicism. Still, he
said, it felt like LARPing each time he tried it. He was seeing good
changes in his life ("objective positive returns" is how Willem
puts it), but still he wanted an experience that would seal his
faith. He was on to Christianity and going no better.

One day he took a walk and spoke to God, telling him that he just needed a sign, something more, to be able to believe in it. Then he rounded a corner and the first thing he saw was a pillar of flame shooting up out of what seemed to be a cauldron. In the next moments he realized he had come to a church that was having some kind of celebration or ritual; there were people gathered on the front lawn around a pot—actually, it really was a cauldron—that had just flared up. From then on God started feeling real.

Nicole gets up and stretches, then gathers up a few empty bottles. I ask Willem if he has any last remarks. He tells me that his perspective on crypto stuff changes all the time. After being immersed in NFTs for about a year, he grew cynical, seeing "trash projects," terrible artworks. Now he thinks we are entering a new historical moment in both art history and tech and that there is an opportunity for artists to make truly original work. He tempers his optimism with one last word of caution, which—in the coming months of escalating crypto crashes—will come to seem comically understated: "It just can't last forever, this perception that everything is gonna go to the moon..."

Staring at someone's face for two hours in a dimly lit room has the effect of making the outside world feel insubstantial. As I walk down the street I wonder what it would take for me to change what I believe in. At 10:45 p.m. on a weeknight, Liberty Petrol, the petrol station on the way to my tram stop, the most beautiful petrol station in Melbourne, looks like something Willem might have designed, glowing red and blue against the white glare of streetlights. The word "Liberty" is lit up in red, and a sign as you drive in says "Welcome to Liberty." It looks like a nostalgic rendering of a petrol station based on some imagined petrol station heyday. Its logo is a two-tone flame that burns twenty-four hours a day.

Acknowledgments

People Who Lunch was first published in Australia by Upswell in 2022. I would like to thank Upswell's publisher, Terri-ann White, who was unfailingly supportive and generous throughout the process — a happy experience for my first book. I'd also like to thank Sophy Williams, who acted as my agent and connected me with Little, Brown Spark, the publishers of this edition. I'm very grateful to Talia Krohn and her team for working with me on the book and for bringing it to an American audience. Thank you to Julianna Lee for the brilliant cover design.

I want to sincerely thank everyone I wrote about in this collection, named or pseudonymed, especially those I interviewed. Without them, the book wouldn't exist.

Justin Clemens, Elizabeth MacFarlane, and Maria Tumarkin all contributed immensely — through feedback and conversations — when they supervised this work in its inception as part of an MA project. In particular, I can't thank Maria enough for helping shape this book in its early stages, and for her ongoing support. I'm grateful for funding from the University of Melbourne and a commissioning grant from the Copyright Agency's Cultural Fund. I'd also like to acknowledge the editors of *SPLM*, Vincent Le and Audrey Schmidt, who published an earlier version of "Good Times in Venice" in 2021. To my comrades in the NTEU and RAFFWU, and to my coworkers for their excitement and support — thank you.

Acknowledgments

I want to thank my writing group—Jack Kirne, Aaron Billings, Ursula Robinson-Shaw, Emma Marie Jones, and Nick Robinson—who were brilliant readers of the essays I workshopped with them. Alex Griffin sifted through at least two of these essays with incredible patience and insight, and I'm humbled by his generosity in doing so. I'm grateful to Neika Lehman, who I shared both a home and an office with for much of the writing process and whose influence is deep in this book. Thank you to Thao Phan, Maria Hach, Amelia Willis, Jade Butler, Necho Brocchi, and Emma Black.

Thank you to my parents for encouraging me to write as a kid, teen, and now adult. Thanks to my grandmother Janice Olds, for publishing me, aged six, using her Apple Macintosh and inkjet printer, and for never letting me forget my early ambitions.

And finally, thank you to Kat Capel. Kat read, reread, and edited essays, talked commas and titles round the clock, and handheld me, literally, through the process of finishing this book. Without Kat—who knows?

About the Author

Sally Olds is a writer from Queensland living in Narrm/Melbourne. Her work has been published by *Sydney Review of Books*, *un Magazine*, AQNB, and the Institute of Modern Art, and collected in several anthologies. *People who Lunch* was short-listed for the Victorian Premier's Literary Awards in 2023 and is her first book.